My Own Religion: The Power of Love

Joseph H. Vertino

NFB
Buffalo, New York

Copyright © 2025 Joseph H. Vertino

Printed in the United States of America

My Own Religion: The Power of Love, Vertino— 1st Edition

ISBN: 979-8-3494-2777-0

Nonfiction> Spirituality
Nonfiction> Religion> Religious Consciousness
Nonfiction> Metaphysics> Religion
Nonfiction> World Religions

A Full Color Version of This Book is Available

ANY part of this book may be RESPECTFULLY USED with a clear declaration of the original author in any format so chosen and deemed appropriate by the user gladly! Please do send a note if you can to the author's party! Thanks
 - Dr. Joe Vertino.

NFB Publishing
119 Dorchester Road
Buffalo, New York 14213
For more information visit Nfbpublishing.com

Archangel Uriel bless us all- the archangel of literature and books.

MY OWN RELIGION: THE POWER OF LOVE

Table of Contents:

1. Being in Love	15
2. Understanding being Human	18
3. Feeling your feelings	24
4. Animals as Leaders	29
5. (Blank)	32
6. The Shadow	34
7. Guru	38
8. Clarity on Religion!	41
9. Power	44
10. My Path toward God	48
11. Karma	51
12. What does it mean to be truly successful?	55
13. The Importance of Adventure	59
14. The Question of Morality	63
15. The Power of Being Weird?	67
16. What is Love, Really?	71
17. Grace, what is it? Why is it relevant?	75
18. What is Soul - Love?	78
19. The Three Jewels	81
20. Nature and its Healing Attributes	88
21. Pain	93
22. The Absence of "Self"	99
23. Relationship(s)	103
24. Organized Religion and God	106
25. Anger, Frustration, and (understanding) Emotions	111
26. Work and Discipline	116
27. Death	121
28. Pets, Animals, and Creatures of All Kinds	128
29. Divine Relationships	135
30. Angels and Spiritual Guides	140
31. Different Relationships and their purpose for our future	147

32. Healing	157
33. Spiritual Entities and how they may matter to you	166
34. Devotion	171
35. Advaita Vedanta/Non-Dual spiritual teachings and teachers	176
36. Attaining and generating balance	180
37. Parenting and Family Relations	186
38. The Importance of Self Expression	193
39. The Importance of Beauty	199
40. Government	203
41. Reiki Healing	208
42. Martial Arts	214
43. Sexuality	221
44. Mental Conditions and altered perspectives	225
45. Music	231
46. Honor (Last segment)	236

PREFACE

About The Author: Hi, I am Dr. Joe, I love God as you will see throughout this manifesto started being written when I was a mere 25 years old in context of how much life experience can be used to put into an only-personal-experience book- I then finished the book when I was 34 years old, January 2025. I have at least 3 more books, ha-ha, they are great and ranging in effect- which is sometimes rare for just ONE Author to achieve!

In loving God and also being a Zen Buddhist I have noticed in all of my passion I never have the tendency to convince anyone of coming out of their own life experience in context of where they are currently as a religious individual- I find it impossible! And I notice myself that these qualities that the "other" possesses about it do not detract from my own; thus the title "My Own Religion:" Further I add a quote as you will see in the book from a famous musician who was very powerful and had a great demonstration publically of his power and talent – that he alone was responsible for – how magnanimous! This book is written in the attempt and inciting attention to that – FORCE! Thus the second half of the title "The Power of Love"

INTRODUCTION

The title of this book requires an explanation; "My Own Religion: The Power of Love" The first half states it is my own, even though I have taken God's wisdom through many influential souls throughout Earth's and other worldly history I filter all of this through my own mind and heart and soul. I feel that is important because I am not going to waste this book's precious pages on repeating words that are boring to type and thus will be boring to read. I AM interested in bringing more light into your mind and emotional experience. I pleasure myself in bringing out the hidden darkness; as Reiki is designed to do with honor and wisdom and presence- as perfect healing is.

I am overjoyed to give wise words to you and to your friends and family perhaps. I enjoy spending my days and nights devoted to God and to the God within you that is holding this holy book. I feel that the holiness of my own being may be able to help you navigate your time on this planet into a more peaceful and overall rewarding life experience. May you find that to be true, I pray! The power of Love is given to me from my family and from my own soul that resonates with these words. I thank you. This is the power of Love, to change your mind for the better and to face the reality of the present moment and the power to heal. Enjoy.

This book is designed in sections or installments that center around one particular topic. If you want to call that "chapters" go ahead. There are 46! –segments like in a beautiful project that take skill to glue together- a wooden toy airplane – may this help you fly your ship of life. References appear with an "*" next to it- throughout the book found at page 185- the info on thee images in this book is found on page 185, and also thee LOG OF MEDIA containing pertinent materials (deeply) correlated with this manifesto "*"!

Note: This is Mother Mary thee ascended master *; if you could look at this image without associating anything to it this would be best for it would be attuning your mind to the Truth, alone, as one's like her did.

1
BEING IN LOVE

What advice and wisdom can I give to you on this? I am in Love, better yet **I am Love**, dead in the water- I have no hope for ever not being that. But some things are just the way they are. I guess you could use this as fodder or kindling for the fires of devotion and ecstasy. Finding some inner truth and shining it into your heart to become magnified into the world around you. Mother Mary is my go-to for this kind of energy, a rapture of sorts. She has said "My soul magnifies the Lord and my spirit rejoices in God my saviour." I don't know how to actually accept this but yet I am writing about that very thing. Who knows? A good question to ask is how does this aid or injure my purpose given to me from divinity to more clearly see and understand my own being.
   I LOVE YOU.

I cannot go into detail on this personally because I have no personal experience! But the energy of Love, the "I am", it is my home vibration! The two beings as seen in the relationship, yes they are part of this divinity, they are who they are and can help each other to realize God through the witnessing of beauty in a pairing of their distinct souls. Thus this basic premise I have come to understand now of being in Love is summed up in a surrender of the mind and also a complete freedom. The mind, from a divine perspective is guiding and witnessing ALL of this. To be yourself is the goal of truly being in Love. To allow God to be perfect as you are.

This is difficult to express without a lot of hand gestures. But the basic idea is that what you are is a perfect gem. You are separate only so that you may understand your own innate perfection! The relationship you may have is serving you to this end, to this divine purpose. I hope and pray that all the bitterness of relationship can cease now and the joy become brighter.

I feel the resonance of my soul and I didn't realize the grandeur of its being. I now know that. I believe that my lover/God and her divine wisdom and enlightened overall purpose is amazing, utterly amazing. I feel that the bounty of Universal Love has its own manner and our confusing experiences in life are not powerful enough to ever prevent that. The absolute has no way of being destroyed, but the illusions can be quite harrowing for us. But, I know in my heart that the grace you need is her. Amen.

The most important aspect, to me, in this chapter is particularly the energy. You may notice it is not weighed down like a blanket that sat in the rain-pour. It is like the sun rays that dried up that blanket. This is a big clue of what the real joy of being released can be felt as in a way of speaking. To feel into an energy that is based in liberation rather than bondage. May the energetic frequency of wisdom prevail!

I guess if we wish to understand more about ourself we can allow ourself to utterly fall in Love and release our tendency to cause harm- It brings more about and Life is meant to come about like a Ship- perhaps that's why they call it a journey! You knowing more and more because of experiences you are meant to be heard and seen just like all those things you see and experience- now this kind of perspective might begin to make sense to your mind why I perceive God in such a way as this; Being in Love. The most powerful way we can love like if we were riding a bike rather than trying to not spill our juice walking over bumps- is like choosing God's Love- the attentiveness and self-trust involved in such a balanced way- that is real and personal- but does not have anxious attachment or wrongful motivations in anyway. Shining is what God wants you to understand rather than anything else in particular that way of Life! And choosing Life is such a sacred thing over and over again- As you do that you may notice the parts of you that were confused may be replaced with Peace and the joyful things. You can make choices with full mind and conscience more as a complete being and then when you choose you can learn to feel good about your choice because it was wholesome and that's it- and the other one, your partner you may be in Love with will eventually have to bow to the Truth just the same one Truth, how simple, exactly as you are getting used to doing when you listen up- this is why God again because that is God's will like your will everyday when put on your boots. God certainly provides more clarity and acceptance the two most important qualities for being in love- with thee other (one).

Bobby Mcferrin- Professional vocalist and exemplar Human (elderly in year 2025- mentioned later in book!)

2
UNDERSTANDING BEING HUMAN

I have called myself a starseed for many years now. If you want to know I feel that I am mostly from Andromeda, the neighboring galaxy that we will merge with in 3 or 6 billion years, approximately. My proof of this is that I have been given some clues and they were not that subtle, but rather quite obvious. I have the eye to spot other Andromedan starseeds. Do you know the alien being from the movie film "E.T. The Extra Terrestrial"? That alien is based on a neonate from the Andromeda galaxy. I have been visited in my dream state by a fellow brother, even though we don't have clear gender lines, so, ~my heart family of the white light of the Cosmic God~, I could say more accurately.

I am prefacing this excerpt with this to reveal my honest and true perspective on the topic of humanity. So, what is being human like? The actual root of the word "human" comes from the 'man of color' being one who has a "hue". But what does it mean to experience life as a human? To be confused, to be misunderstood, to be vulnerable beyond comparison? To be the hope for other races perhaps?

There is a being named Bashar* who is channeled by Darryl Anka who is from our future timeline and comes from a place called Essassani, the place of living light. They have taken this name because they are completely based in love and Light and they want to help us out but they also are from OUR future timeline, which means we will be with them in the future. So, that is hopeful. They say humanity is very exciting because we represent the nexus and pinnacle or zenith for all these different and involved alien races some of which are more obvious like ET or the grays and others are more subtle, like the plasma beings who apparently live inside of the Earth on a different dimensional plane - that I heard of from an awesome guide named "Drunvalo Melchizedek" *. How lovely.

But, is being human so different from all the other life forms in existence? Or is it that we are different for a divine reason and purpose? The common threads (also the name of one of my favorite Bobby Mcferrin* songs) is essential. What is common ground for all of us here on Earth? "WE" as opposed to just "I". We are a community of individual peoples. We are all different even to each other but we can live in harmony and peace- those differences are so important and encouraging each day- so they aren't the problem, you can be certain- in fact the evil way which is utterly possible is in the opposite direction of respect, encouragement, acknowledgement, and gratefulness and hopefully enjoyment of all possible differences- Hitler is a clear example.

We have been aware of what it takes for us to thrive for many thousands of years. But we have been interfered with and it takes intense awareness become beyond our fears based in differences and to see the Love in all our differences. We can see that God created all of us differently so that we may better glorify life. We may cause more pain if we choose to but we may also ALL choose to move into a heart based reality in which we move out from the land of perpetual judgments and into the paradiso magnificat. This is my hope for all of us. I believe that my awareness of galactic energies can be helpful and useful to Earth vibes- like when Yogi's point their hands in prayer to the sky- and allow and encourage a natural smile to come about. This is also like connecting heaven with the Earth as is inevitable this connection so why not practice Tai Chi Qi Gong and Yoga about it!

We may use our energy body to commune with God as a cosmic awareness and love to heal and aid the future progress and harmony of this planet at this time in our collective understanding of history. We will only be able to do this if we trust in God or whatever you would like to call it. Children are already doing this. The kids on this planet are all involved in the evolution of humankind and many of them may resonate with galactic energies. We can see the tensions on this planet can be relieved by a more expansive and passive means of existing that may be available to us from other realms or levels of consciousness.

So, I highly recommend you do not ignore the bi-product of the words here in this passage, they are based in a deep unconditional and galactic form of Love which we are perpetually included in and have people like thee author to show us thanks to thee internet- but ultimately and most importantly we must experience it first hand alone as our own person always is- perhaps the biggest clue on "understanding being human". Thanks.

> There ARE beings that are overjoyed to be open to us on, sincerely, every level, I am One.

You may want to look into researching channeling on YouTube despite what the Catholic Church says about these things. YOU are responsible for finding your own way; that should be exciting! YOU are a perfect being that is beyond comparison and comprehension and only when you meditate on God will you find these channels into cosmic awareness opening. I pray you may be guided! Perhaps we know this because the channelers can attest to it- and we are all made the same as humans- we have the same capacity and these channelers are just one of us. Darryl Anka mentioned on page 5 is sincerely a proud channeler, he was great!

I did not plan, when I started typing this excerpt, to write so obviously and openly about other life forms available to us. But, to make it clear, the remedy for fearing the unknown is the lynchpin or the crux of this post. We all have experienced God's love and desire to be loved and to eventually Love the way God loves all Being (in some way?). So, with this being said, it may be overwhelming to consider galactic energies but when you are in love with God or any being that fear of the unknown becomes an excitement by way of transmutation.

For example, when you stare at your beloved in the eyes you can be hopeful that he or she will reveal some hidden part of them that you can quickly put into your heart and cherish for all eternity. The alchemy of Love is at work in this experience. The most clear way of perceiving humanity as a healer is through the understanding of the chakra system and in the Reiki lineage and desire to heal. I feel that the white light of universal awareness, as God's own light, is open and available to all of humanity at this time in our evolution.

I have been using Reiki for many years or perhaps lifetimes and I plan on it only growing larger in my openness towards everyone. The general good will of Reiki is abundant and ever available. I feel that music is a primordial trait that can be used to bring people together in the heart center.

There are commonalities, but what does it mean to actually BE human in itself and in completion? To be honest, I suppose. There are many ways of living a life and humanity probably is the most varied planet of intelligent life that is not yet cosmic fairing, I would make my case for that in some heavenly courtroom. I feel that maybe even humans don't know what being human really is. That perhaps is why I am writing and you are reading this. I believe that there are societal constructs but are they what we prefer? Do we think everything would become barbaric if we collapsed our governmental systems? I have the courage to find out for my-own-self the way to do that is not in destroying building and corporations or anything that can be used for goodness like a government for sure- but what needs destruction is never those things- I guess my human-self is someone who is willing to destroy those blockages.

I decided years ago that I would be myself and find out if I was truly so good or evil. You can see that there is a greater desire for Truth than there is to "fit into" society consistently, and further society is still quite questionable at its core to me personally. Soren Kierkegaard* said "With great freedom comes great anxiety". What did he mean to tell us here? He said this from his own heart, he was a follower of Jesus and he said this too... that is progress, it means he is not blinded by his belief system in a way that is clear to me - he, Soren, is soaring above the clouds of lingering pains and is resounding his gong which is the barest truth.

He is saying that if we had the power to travel the cosmos alone as a planet in a great big ship (which is what is already going on pretty much) we could go anywhere, that would be stellar but the people I assume would feel somewhat anxious on this first step outward. Do I think that is a good idea for us to fly away? No! Do I think we should first understand our motivations? Yes! And can we apply that to a microcosmic perspective? We can. Let's do that:

When a child goes out of their house for the first time is a fair example. The child moves into the unknown expanse of their neighborhood and sees the trees, and the grass, and the people with their other children and/or dogs walking around. This is very exciting but can cause some unrest or anxiety in us if we are not spiritually prepared and rooted to encounter the newness of our external reality. So, maybe, we could conclude- that Soren's idea of Freedom is overly generalized and is an *aspect* of freedom not the entire thing. But, once you begin on the path of true freedom you become more open to new experience and you become more faithful and trusting which basically cancels out anxiety. The path of true freedom is not something that comes and goes like anxiety does but true freedom enables an individual to fully experience anxiety and then still get to make choices over and over again. Yay, God.

For example, when we are moving through experiences with our physical form we are still in touch with a still and deep essence I call God. **SO,** what are our motivations? We have left our common room and housing situation. We are exploring by our own means and ways. We can be honest

With ourself outside, we are here, to put it bluntly, to BE FREE (er). Is there an exciting option available externally right now? Is there a means to an end in context?

Carrying on; God is a universal Truth and subjective Truth combined into one point. I like to see this as Reiki energy. The most common aspect I have found for humanity is a quiet or sometimes chaotic longing. For what, it is hard to say off the top of my head. I believe that when we surrender to Love we can begin to explore that. God bless you humanity.

What music has taught me is that the universal can certainly be used to put bickering to rest, hopefully for good. The Universal expanse has no bias toward us, albeit our differences. The sound or vibration of creation is something that is beyond our known areas of existence. On this Earth we all know music as vibration, the culture we are born into decides that for us, for the most part.

The reason I am discussing this is if we are looking at the overarching Truth of humanity we shall find some answer in the consistent. Music is a global if not a Universal phenomenon or experience. Some would say that to understand what it means to be human is only possible through an outside source. Others would say the reverse, what IS the self-given definition of 'human'? I am human now so I will answer it.

> <u>I believe</u> that humanity is a certain perspective that has a collective pull or vibration based in belonging and a desire to be loved, known, and heard.

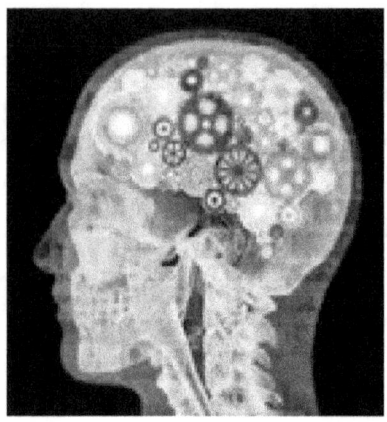

3
FEELING YOUR FEELINGS

Warning ... suicide discussed here. (For adults)

This is not a death note, it is the light of Hope for those who never got to speak about the pain of Life and ended theirs. I hope and pray that you understand. This segment is a glaring success in one way alone which is its allowance of these perturbing feeling to have the stage, to be at the forefront and to remain there and to allow the enormity of your Spirit to work a wonder of awareness and healing by proving its completion and superiority over attachment of pain really in your life experience.

Really what is going on in this post is a cathartic experience it is not purely scientific but the resonance of it is surely sincere. Enjoy.

It is always important to process our feelings. A great place for this is in the bath. I don't know how to stop the mind as it races towards GOD'S HEART. But as we sit and steep like good tea bags in our emotional state we can trust in God to create some kind of serenity for us every time. I was suicidal yesterday. It is not something that solves much but you know you have nothing to lose at this point. I remember a story of a high school boy hero who was so kind that he literally could not stand this place because the circumstances he experienced were so ignorantly unkind and he ended his lifetime, God bless him. I don't think this is a good sign for you, humanity. I think you need to get your act together and start dancing and singing in the streets and to listen to more "Rage against the Machine." I recommend "Bulls on Parade " and "Guerilla Radio". *

So, when we have extended ourselves too far we end our lives because we literally have no more energy to continue. I'm pretty certain that happens to me on a regular basis. It's funny I am still writing this book. But I guess this will create some kind of legacy of Love after I am out of here, dead and gone. I am not planning on committing suicide, by the way, I am referring to the time on Earth following my death of natural causes. I pray that all the people reading this who have felt suicide in their veins can find some kind of Love and Light now. I think of the Buddhists who self- immolated their corporeal forms. I don't know maybe they felt too cold, or that this planet could use more fire. I love you too you bald headed saints (?) of pastimes... So, I usually would say "Get enlightened first then consider suicide more seriously" Or you could just completely scrap everything and start your life over again and/or both. Intentional communities are cool.

My take on suicide is that maybe enlightenment is a form of suicide. The death process itself is seen and then you perceive a more accurate representation of yourself as eternal. Imagine next time you are suicidal that during bath time you are being born again. Jesus committed suicide in his heart in the sense that he knew that his sacrifice was the most ridiculous and ballsy form of Love at that specific time when we as humans were so stuck in blind acts of violence.

There was a man named Zen Master Rama*. He apparently committed suicide after becoming a somewhat controversial spiritual teacher. He is one of my absolute favorite people, because I truly believe that sentiment "Your light and your being was too simple, gracious and subtle for this world, and it was going on to the next" is basically referring to Zen master Rama. I believe he knew something special, he knew that suicide doesn't't actually rid you of your pain body. You owe that knowledge to your soul and its growth.

<u>The important point is that you as a being understand that life as it is is unescapable because you are it. You as a soul are here for a lifetime and you learn through ALL Thee experiences of life and come to acquire knowledge throughout ALL of your incarnations.</u> The logical conclusion, is that suicide it comes up from time to time as an "option" it isn't ... one. But we can see that as life we are in a place of endearing sincerity on Earth as humans and have a great love for flowers.

We are also usually adept at walking around. To this moment it is a remnant of my soul's growth and its healing process, so that I could heal you too. I guess you could connect this darkness to my other book "The Nothingness of Love : A Buddhist Book of Poetry" LOG OF MEDIA*I believe that the healing perspective on this is that you could say my soul is the wounded healer. The desire for non-existence arising from a painful experience, but what of the joy? At least I didn't say the word over and over gain : SUICIDE- it is a linguistic paradox because the word itself would kill my tongue my whole being so it is the only word I will ever reject, I cannot abide with you. But to give respect to you, this word, I have said you once and I am respectful and demand respect so for the sake of his sorrowful passion the Lord- the reading is implying your damn meaning- but once.

I guess that's something we can look into, the abyss. The opening of the infinite heart of compassion, you might be like the buddhists ones and see shapes as they did. Do you know of the Sri Yantra*? It is a buddhist holy symbol they apparently saw collectively in deep states of meditation. Apparently you may need something like a symbol to help you open up your heart space. They feel this symbol is useful to us. I feel that they did not all go into nirvana somewhere in Tibet when the serpent of Light was expressed in that location because they had more soul work to do, meaning in this case, balancing their prejudices and revealing them. So, a good spiritual exercise is this: ~instead of casting out your judgments as demons to open your heart into them.~

Moving through each experience as if you were going through space in the Millennium Falcon with Chewbacca as your guide. Connect with the earth and explore your mind alone in the dark, then in the bath, in the bedroom, and in

your heart. Finding some true serenity at letting go of all that garbage, trust Mother Earth if you want to feel some relief. You'll see she doesn't care what you believe as much as "Jesus" * does. I use quotes because we have a fake Jesus epidemic going on. People don't want to know the Truth of Jesus Christ, they think they do because they are unfortunately severely confused.

This can be healed only with an opened hearted and joy filled zen mind. This is a neutral place to operate from and to be truly humble. Be weak to eventually become strong. Spa with the Lord, in the Light. Be completely honest and open. Hate the Lord, that would be a better choice than hiding in your rectories. The real devotees of Christ exist in the shadows because they shine too bright for your societally blind eyes.

I have mentioned somewhere in the future of this book that emptiness is the relief from judgment. For example, we can take a breath in complete surrender to the emptiness before we enter that courtroom that we think is our life and death and payed for our lunch, meaning to put our lifetime into perspective. There are people who exist that can heal you instantly, did you know that? There is a dog that can lick your face once and can heal your entire ancestral lineage. I don't know how I know this but it's true, to me. But, I do appreciate the Reiki healers on the planet called Earth also. So, as we move along through our experiences of Earth life it might just happen out of the blue.

A homeless man's eyes see you and you weep in joyful healed surrender and divine acceptance. So, my friend said to me "What are you going to do when no one else needs healing?" Well, I am sure I will have a random thought and then sleep on it. And then nothing really will change, so, go figure.

Feeling your feelings, or rather feeling THEE feelings. When we depersonalize them they disappear after we have studied them well enough and we are what we are forever. As a conscious being of Love. Forever Love. Ram Rama Ram. I recommend you research a woman, a present day Saint named "AMMA"*. **I do love you, and I want you to be fully alive!**

Om nam myoho renge Kyo!* I am upholding the cosmic law, beyond comings and goings. The ten thousand and one things are irrelevant to this eternal presence of divine hearted Love. Lotus flowers are blooming. . .

As you may have sensed throughout this segment my life has been very difficult and agonizing obviously unnecessarily- That justice seems so far away on every level and it lasts and stings you when it wants to that reality. And you may come to find there is just no lesson there in it- except for just you. Thee feelings that seem to haunt and the beginning of that kind of sufferings surrender is enabled by the simple recognition of just yourself that happens to be present all the time- and as you continue to live, and thank God for your life, The light starts to manifest in the center of it all- your heart chakra. Your life punishment of penance can be found to be meaningless on a level of the intellect and then you may suddenly become just grateful about just having a one mind. And the root of suicide that is a somehow convincing one- "I am inherently a piece of shit" can be traded for a simple rock or stone on your journey of Life.

A wolf in the snow not quite just the sunlight.

4
ANIMALS AS LEADERS

If animals were seen in a different light by humans we could see the value of this perspective. Allowing animals to lead us in a way would be refreshing because animals are more authentic… they do what they do and that's it. When they relax they fully relax when they fight they fully fight. But they can teach us what it truly means to be oneself because they are undoubtedly that.

When someone is journeying into their own divinity they come across all of the beliefs that disturb them and injure their inner child. These beliefs are formations that can be melted away with self-love. And the paradox of self-love is that it is relevant just as much as the aspect of enlightened consciousness as "no self"-ness. Refer to * "Chapter 22: Absence of Self" Page 65.

The Native American people understood the importance of animal spirit when they would make totem poles. They would choose specific animals for specific spiritual empowerment rituals. This is a good relationship with nature because it is based on mutual respect and equality. It is also deepened when the Great Spirit or God is brought into the ritual space.

The lion is the king of the animal realm for a very important reason. The king Lion has the heart that is the biggest and as we live our lives we can make conscious decisions to expand our heart space. The king Lion rules with the heart not the ego mind, the big awareness not the little ego. This is the shining archetype of true leadership and Kinghood. So, I feel that the animals must develop a sense of respect for one another. As we grow as individuals we interact with many beings big and small and learn many new ways; possible ways we can exist.

But we must be accountable for ourself because when we go out into the world we, as an individual, are leading our own life, blazing our own trail deep into the forest of our personhood and also to God's own heart of Light. We alone can surf the waves and we alone can swim to shore. We learn the importance of finding a community based in unconditional love. In which we can manifest safety and dreams based on excitement and true family hood.

The "general faultiness of our self" inside of us which hopefully did not escape the stage of a zygote and become a conscious manifestation in our mind- us and it alone. This manifestation is not true inherently it is something that is a painful experience and lead to suicidality, but that is thee only TRUTH that there is inside of it, which may be seeming like something worth holding inside of us like a mother holds her son or daughter inside of herself. The Feng shui of the universe on the other hand is not something we can even grasp with a stick or a net or a photo or a book- it is never available for our grasping and is always on the outside - of our ... self (puts hands across heart). The glowing nature of our hearts is something like a miracle which we can feel and sense but we in that are not separate from it, so there is no inside or outside to that.

Whilst we are beckoned outside of our physical shelters regularly over and over again what a depressed many that would become if there were no sun-to-forehead personal experiences when it was called upon by God to occur - for the first and not last time, amen. This unspeakable but seemingly shakeable bond between all of us and (the divinity) of nature allows for more of us and less of lying. It allows for more of us using our eyeballs and and less of everything else. It allows for more of clarity in context of every little thing we could ever possibly believe in our mind alone, as one person in one very lifetime, and less of the meanderings or lack-of-conclusions whilst certainty as potential is a constant companion- for ethics sake, to be clear.

The justice of Animals as Leaders as a guiding principle of one's own personal life is so profoundly saving specifically and perhaps alone - saving us from this "general faultiness in our self"- this harrowing comparison that enters our scope, our periphery, perhaps, as a drunk dose- and as we that a bolt of grace and turn our head like a bird to see a bird actually in real life - we are seeing through any comparison and therefore the root of this disgusting potential habit of our mind becomes eradicated forever- saved by nature- and it was IN THE IMITATION AND NOT ANYTHING ELSE- WE ARE SAVED. Which is to say- a proud and childish choice, a pure one; but do not dismayed by my choice of words on it my earth; Animals as leaders! To be so respectful as to see them how see our world leaders- to give them a bow and to be receptive to their word even if we do not know their tongue- be proactive in context of survival alone and to know how lucky and lovely we are as humans for we get to perceive all these animals not just one and pick and choose which we will see today in our mind and allow the entirety of the mind to be there in the WONDER of this one animal- and knowing how great it is to be alive and to know your past, which included your SELF-HATE and to see the proudest moment any heart chakra can ever see- which is yourself happy on the Earth- evermore. I love you- a wise man I am.

5
(Blank)

Good day soul seeker. Or maybe you are a soul finder. Ha-ha. So. I would like to discuss the idea of reality being an illusion. So, this taken at face value is a paradox of the highest regard. Because it is a contradiction. But, I say we can make some sense of this with love as our companion and guide.

When the yogis of the ancient paths would commune with the Lord in deep reverence and meditation they would see the moon and stars inside themselves AS themselves.

This makes one understand the statement that the external world may not be so real. But then one can see the inverse as well. For example, when I am empty I see and feel love for all about me and in my environment, so in that moment I feel "me" as inside is not as real as what is perceived with love around me. I also feel that love is what is ultimately reality. A quote that clarifies and satisfies: "wisdom tells me I am nothing, love tells me I am everything and between these two my life flows." -Nisargadatta Maharaj. *

So, when we see that substance is mostly empty space we can begin to have a shift in perception. Quantum physicists know this; they know that an atom is mostly empty space. So what does that mean for our existence? It means that we are more than just some physical universe that we are nothing but something and so the spiritual quest endures.

So, another Indian sage, Ramana Maharshi*, was interested and determined to find out the truth of his existence. He laid down on the ground and imagined death, he transcended the illusion and woke up to a deeper reality. But this reality is based in silence, it is something that we can talk around but to experience it we must have a combination of God's grace and a pure desire for Truth which he had, that sage.

His student was Papaji*, and his student is Mooji who is a very popular sage and is on youtube, a very cool guru figure.

So, to conclude; the concept of emptiness is not against the stuff of existence. But rather it is based on a mutually beneficial relationship as all duality is... hot then cold, empty and full. They are interdependent. Yin yang. If you wish for a spiritual and gratitude based perspective ~ seek the stillness within the movement, itself.

6
THE SHADOW

The shadow self is an important aspect of our consciousness. I firmly believe the inner child uses the shadow to protect its innocence, when seen this way it begins to open up the heart and releases any hidden judgments. We can see the light as direct or truthful and the darkness as clouded or sometimes willingly deceptive. So, both emanate from the heart, when one feels love there are deep reasons for any choice that people make including if they wish to be negative or positive. But to me what is essential is God's love. This love is real and is unmistakable when someone can see it working. To me this is one of my great Joy's and hobbies is to witness how God's Love moves and is changing things for the better; bringing some clarity, wisdom, and miracles of healing.

A lot can be said and already has been said about one's shadow side by Teal Swan*. She is a great source. So, the shadow may be willingly deceptive to get what it wants but what it wants may not be so dark or evil. What it wants might just be straight up love, unconditional love + "Baby, don't hurt me— don't hurt NO MORE". But people misunderstand this, they try to shoot love at it and heal and transform it too soon before the shadow has been accepted for what it is fully- we cannot fake LOVE ever it is never possible but we surely can tell the Truth as I am here and now. That you Lord for being my rock I know you and you let me AND once I started I was lead by you so deeply and allowed me to be a penetrating force as a true man through each stepping place- and by your grace and your waves of bliss as an option from time anyway or night to day for hours on end or blink awake like with Eckhart Tolle like his final morning as it began his enlightenment that stayed he is surely proud of his life onwards it became.

Thank you for all the souls that are responsible for Teal Swan's well being - she surely is a Spiritual Catalyst- a part of it all that belongs to no one it seems but if I could I give it all I could and would give it in front of enemies walking to her arms the house that is all the goods humanity needs generally- seems like a joke it is not one and never will be no matter how people laugh or from whatever angle they sit or stare at my dear words about her alone that TEAL SWAN.

Acceptance is a great form of unconditional LoVe that is very necessary. The benefit of enlightened consciousness is this: that the true guru accepts unconditionally what is given to his or her experience.

The shadow is transformed when it becomes really accepted by the heart and then we are open to grace rather than a struggle. And then we begin to honor the past negativity and use our mind and soul to create WITH the heart. This opens doors to the unknown realms of awareness and bliss. Perhaps the SHADOW is like an impasse. This I pray you can feel. Since this topic requires honesty, let us know that full well. There is an interesting song on my mind I remember performing from school… "Tu Lo Sai"* . This song was and is Italian it is basically about a cruel situation and how this plays into the shadow is that the revealing of the truth can bring about great transformation.

In this song... the lyric is:

"You know full well..." So, One person who is experiencing life through their own shadow may truly be in the place of the character in this song... after the fact of their cruelty has occurred.

A FASCINATING idea is that the shadow may be only made possible through the carrying through of intentional or unintentional harm done to a person. And then its (the shadow) purpose we have already outlined and then the remedy is to allow the truth to be made present.

And now a musical comes to mind is "Jesus Christ Superstar" *There is a parable of sorts that is applicable. In this musical Jesus is bringing light to the minds of other souls that have incarnated near him we could assert to be near to him in this very life. And to the point, the shadow is like sometimes a thick covering on the innocent face and those who truly live and see are the proper ones to help those who are suffering needlessly. LOG OF MEDIA – SONG * from musical found on page 182.

As a light bringer myself I enjoy sharing this point: That the shadow is an inevitability that is unnecessarily domineering in the face of the Truth; our Truth objectively and scientifically- of our shared world and universe. This revelation is somewhat of a boon or savior to our encapsulated self because it is not a move in anyone's arsenal to attempt to remove an inherent aspect of our life, even though it may seem like a good idea it is not it is simply an ultimately personal inner cloistered (recurring) experience that is only exposed partly and is and cannot sink the whole ship of our entire being- but it has a pull a gravitas; it is an aspect of the Spirit to be open and honest but we must also rest well and to do that we must not forfeit our qualities of safety for the sake of an illusory interior battle. The shadow is like smoke and please don't attempt to pick up a weapon against it and its will!

The will of this shadow is not against anything or everything that you are but it is like I wrote an inevitability of consciousness as a human being- the reason that is so important to truly know is because we MUST know it comes from only within ourself- for it is our business alone.

It is not another person or entity we can engage with but is something we don't need to take any STANCE AGAINST AT ALL. And simply allow its nature to float- and the purpose of it to come into our experience which is the rawest education possible! If you want to know the TRUTH OF IT. It projects by way of universal laws thus the word used gravitas: It has no possibility of being managed or manipulated but is ultimately selfish in its raw grounding; and needy intention in which way alone it is purely contextual- Simply being willing to see for yourself is enough. Amen .

Neem Karoli Baba- maharaj

Thank you to all the guru's throughout the ages -Ram ram. [[<< >>]]

7
GURU

The "guru" is a word that loosely translates as "darkness to light" or otherwise someone who brings the individual or collective consciousness from a dark place to a light place. I believe that yes one has to be unequivocally established in the light of God to do this successfully and normally. But I also feel it is important to say that the dark states are bridged with unconditional love and when we move through them into the bridge we may transcend them into the light. I feel that this is seen when Krishna Das talked about his guru * Neem Karoli Baba. He said that there wasn't anything they did, like meditate, or pray, or do yoga but there was just the love of God constantly. Like it was sunbathing in the aura of God.

I have been communing with this saint for some years and have had many great experiences through his grace and presence. Just today my dog gave me infinite kisses as she does from time to time (when God calls for them)- also I pray that children and old men don't count the kisses that dogs give to us- so that we may instead befriend infinity. I was meditating and praying in song with Krishna Das and Hanuman – reference the image * at the beginning of Chapter 34: devotion, page 127 in this great book (please share it with friends) at the beginning of Chapter and I felt that God appointed my dog and Neem Karoli Baba to clean my heart. Thank you for that. I felt all of the darkness of my past weeks moving through me into the great warm heart of my guru figure. My man. I feel that this transmutation and healing cleansing is part of the job of a guru.

The beings that come to them are attracted to the Truth in them. The God-ness in one is attracted to the God-ness in another. The one who is the guru is fully embodying this vibration of God's love and enlightenment.

When the student or seeker sits with the master they begin to relinquish levels of illusion over many years or even lifetimes of disappointment because now they feel safe at last. Then the healing and atonement begins. The real work of salvation and God can become active rather than passive at this time.

So, it is so important to know the Truth preferably as Children about this topic! Guru is appropriate to think of as someone who has climbed their own rungs so to speak- and knows so much their own self and the ladder to heaven itself. And it has been so ordained that no other being shall be who they are and they make sure to guard the souls against the illusions of the mind because only they can- a very appropriate thing to have in perspective all life long- A general benevolence towards singled out beings for the reason those beings are singled at all is a great foundational constant we can instill in our entire species- the lineage of Guru as an ever proud figure being revered is an orderly stabilizing gift to realize. So, ultimately the correct building of character… made more popular through the GURU. The guru is mostly an establishment of DEEP TRUST in one person who is obviously not the Guru. The divine relationship dawns and the soul can be grounded and tethered to a communal Truth inside in Spirit represented forever outside by this one other person who is that Guru!

So the Truth is the Guru removes the darkness and shows us we do not KNOW everything and we do not need to know that- which is the nature of Light to reveal even unto who knows not we are in and under a need to be saved by just a revelation done by Light.

It's strange to allow God to take the form of a teacher. We are so accustomed to God being a mysterious force that exists but it is hard to pin it down so when we feel that from one heart in front of us we are in an adjustment period. This takes time for people to accept. I would hope that a true student may completely trust the true teacher; sadhguru. As someone who is considered a teacher, I pray that my students can learn to trust me! So, essentially the only 'hope for enlightenment' (a great song by Jean-Phillipe Rykiel and Lama Gyurme which can be found in thee LOG OF MEDIA -*) is when the trust in the Love is the focal point. And then the surrender happens all on its own. To see this more clearly. We are bound to an experience and with each step there is a deeper penetration of the experience, as it is. And now the next logical step is not suffering or further struggle, it is complete acceptance. Thank you for reading. Hope this helps you. God hugs. Amen. **Lord Buddha bless us all.**

> P.s. If you ever confused in Life refer back to this last prayer (in bold above)

Jesus Christ/Yeshua thee Ascended Master (also from "my" Reiki Course)

8
CLARITY ON RELIGION!

So, the point of most of my work is to heal the wounds of division between religions that have seemed exclusive and separate for the greater part of our history.

For some years now I have felt that a large part of my soul mission is to do exactly what I aim to do with these words in this post. So, this has been a long time coming. I was born into a Lutheran church and eventually through my own vision came into the realm of open thought and philosophy. As I encountered existentialism I shook hands with atheism and nihilism. I later came to MY OWN understanding of the universe, God, the soul, and nirvana.

I no longer accepted things as others would have me see them but rather as my own heart demanded I do so. I feel that the most transcendental religion is Japanese Zen Buddhism as experienced with and through Reiki energy healing. The reason for this is because it has no baggage. There is no dogma or belief system. This is why Reiki is in alignment with God and healing because it does not contribute to further sufferings. So, the big religions are Christianity, Buddhism, Hinduism, Taoism, Islam, Judaism/Kaballah and many more but these I have first hand experience with in this life enough to write in my manifesto.

I see these religions or belief systems as complimentary in the greater understanding when seen from a more real, understanding, or humble perspective. How would you see religion if you were God? All religion is an attempt to capture the divine, but only when you release the victim of divinity from his/her captivity into the open space of your cosmic mind do you truly know the truth and joys of freedom.

For example, when I was a child I would ritually experience unconditional love and peace. It came from nowhere and returned to nowhere- and thinking back on it as a professional SPIRITUAL GUIDE it certainly wouldn't contribute to the ego of my parents, haha. This is innocence and is before any mental structures that we could possibly manifest. When we begin to see the religions are part of this cosmic entity we call consciousness we begin to heal our minds. We secretly crave relief almost all the time. The ultimate relief is to be one with Love or the Lord's energies- music is a great blessing to this end- in the LOG OF MEDIA - you can find my (author as musician) personal recorded music (soundcloud) *. This is not dependent on anything and cannot be forced or even destroyed. This to me is the hope for humanity. A cloud of love that is beyond our inconveniences and that is ultimately nourishing and enriching.

This is the foundation but it is so ephemeral. We must respect reality and cannot force it into ourselves or others or anything at all. I feel the most important goal for my writing this besides healing in general is to find my own authentic voice. All people possess something that is unique and cannot be copied anywhere by anyone else in all the universes.

This to me is the greatest gift we could be offered and I am here to help with that specifically. The way I have put it is if you know God loves you then why worry. And if you feel there is no God then why worry also. So, when we see that the beliefs we hold are temporary placeholders for a pure Zen reality check then we become humbled, hopefully, very quickly.

To me the grace be able to accept anything most important question is now: <u>why is silence not enough?</u> What this means is just what it means. Thank you for being yourself.

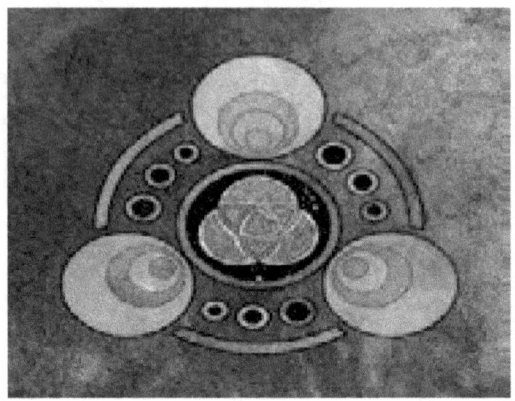

Arcturian Starseed Art

9
POWER

It seems when people get the power they end up abusing it. This is an issue that I hope to remedy with a quote; "When the love of power gives in to the power of LoVe the world will know peace" - Jimi Hendrix (paraphrased)*. So, I would say that this is a general phenomenon that applies to the universal conception of "power". So, now picking apart the quote, at the heart of it all is a sense of denial. When someone has a difficult time with the present moment they resort to unruly behavior; meaning that this behavior is unbecoming of a ruler.

So, I would offer a solution of epic proportions. Community. When someone, anyone, feels important to those who are important to them they feel safe and they feel as if they belong in that community. But, a true community will never fall to the ego. A true community requires exactly the appropriate amount of work and strength and "struggle" to thrive.

So, when people begin prioritizing this all of the egos will fall away. This is what a monastery is supposed to be. A place where people can fully focus on the divine BUT where the monasteries and convents have gone off track is because they have secretly ego-grasped the Truth, or at least attempted to.

The people that are really meant to be in charge will be, in time. Speaking for myself, I personally feel that whether I am a ruler or not I will conduct myself the same. I believe in who I am as relevant, important, and of good character. But the best relief for me is that my joy is not dependent on this. I can be content with watching the grass grow. I enjoy being.

The basis of all things is being. But more specifically being Love.

So, the interesting phenomenon I have also observed is that those who are truly loving sometimes seem to take the most punishment. This has to stop. Just because someone happens to love you unconditionally doesn't mean we should test out their pain tolerance because we cannot understand them and their ways of endless acceptance. And who knows they may also have the power over your very existence.

I don't always know the right answers but as a leader, I know that that is not as much as an issue as resolving conflicts and trusting in God. Sometimes, the true leader has to exemplify immense courage when no one will act they must. And also when no one will stop they must stop. This is leading by example and remaining focused on a goal when people become aimless. There is a time for purposeless floating and there is time for grit and determination, and there is a time for Zen, always.

The great questions can be boiled down to a simple yet difficult question, are you being moved by fear or by LoVe? This is something we must face, and we must face it alone. When we are ready to grow, we will.

So, recapitulating on my first point, the move to power is not wrong in its essence but at some point, you can wake up and make choices for yourself. And when you make the right choices you become superhuman.

You become invincible because you are evolving consciously from a paradigm of mindless choices to more mindful ones. You are deciding for yourself... that is different from what we have learned in a conditioned mind, isn't it? We haven't necessarily heard that come from authority much if at all. But as someone who is actually interested in the well-being of all people, that includes you, I say that we have to first be willing and ready to be great then once we make that first completely personal choice we begin to foster an external reality that works with that shift inside.

I would prefer that everyone might experience nirvana. I would prefer that everyone might feel completely loved. I would prefer that everyone would have a glimpse of what real family is. I would prefer that everyone have the opportunity for immense growth and to share their gifts with others to inspire them on their personal journey. I would prefer that everyone enjoy receiving and giving respect.

> ~The person that is willing to surrender their power at any moment is the one who is truly worthy of ruling!~

The interesting point of this kind of writing is that it is very idealistic and hopeful and intense but I feel that there is a lot of energy that I am drawing from, I dare say that energy is an infinite reservoir or source; God itself. I feel that God takes care of those that have the right way. I know that saying things like "the right way implies a wrong way, which is true but the more important thing is that you see how love does not shrink away when someone is going down the wrong path because LoVe is a deep reality and can never be minimized or replaced, but you must look into the center of your being and find your balance point. That is why YOU are who you are because YOU can never be minimized or replaced. There is no other being in all of the realms of consciousness that IS precisely you, at this moment, AS this moment. Be One with that.

Last night I sat with a new friend; I love conversation and enjoyed my POWERFUL Speech with that other person. I was very adamant about coming to thee intellectual completest understanding about Empowerment in that hour or so. Understanding is such a logical thing that it can be seen step by step what it really is- and once you get it it never runs away from you and Logic; once you get that it provides you with the supplement your soul craves which is everything based in the Truth!

So, what is empowerment really? It is something that is the most precious to obtain- It has an unquenchable desire and sheer willingness constantly to manifest. It allows the experience of life to be an active engagement on an individual level and supersedes the nefarious agenda of anything other than its true divine nature. It is the empowered person who does not fall prey to the seeming necessity of bigotry or oppression, and but the closest the empowered person would go is into a momentous clarification of selfhood preventing the crimes from manifesting through them alone.

The joy that we all need is found only from empowerment; because it is taking our energy and making choices that are giving of more Life based in creation even though a literal choice of it may be something that completely shuts out the world- It is by the genuine engagement with selfhood that results in the permanent recognition of all's potential! Thee undying nature of the Great eternal Light is set in stone ahead constantly and is as a clear Path – obviously unto me the Great Spiritual teacher and now obvious to you. The swelling of the goodness in Pride only comes to fruition through listening in some strong way to my words!

The unfortunate scientific fact is that- I am clear say Life that I can develop through laziness to be a disempowered being – that meets its inevitable end also- and sees the same sidewalk as the birds who swing their wings and yell out without doubtlessness today in the Earth! The desire for sleep should not carry on like your cooking pot trying to balance it on your head through the day. The entire life is pure power and you are such a mystical one that you can be swooned and graceful in its wake and essence- this is all truly about being empowered. This you are reading this because you deserve to know the Truth!

10
MY PATH TOWARD GOD

Philosophy: the scientific study and love of truth. I have been in love with Truth my entire life. When I was a child I would observe. I would sit in my own space and would just be. This was enough for me and I feel it is the core of my spirituality and relationship with God. I have been open minded and open hearted my whole life and have enjoyed being different. Prayer is a personal experience. When someone is invested in prayer he or she begins an energetic journey towards God the path toward God is one that is as unique as you are. You may see that one day when you look back at your steps. I feel that it is important for seekers to know that because it reveals the truth as raw rather than manufactured. For example, if we feel there is only one right way - we will be full of gall and audacity. But if we see that God knows how to bring people to him or herself perfectly-we let go of our personal agenda and we transcend our limited beliefs in exchange for a mind after the mind of God.

I know in my soul and heart that God is inherently perfect. And in that position of knowing you can become a living miracle that God works through. To me I see the love of God as the most influential energy in the cosmos. When we spend time in the vast expanse of God's heart we begin to soften our edges and we listen to the voice within that eventually dominates our hearts when we fall in love with it. I have often heard that people desire to be possessed by God. And I suppose that's for the better when we allow God to be fully empowered and have our full attention and devotion.

The wonderful only way for anyone to come to God – is by themselves- it can never be with anyone else. It has such a ring to it like when you are listening to the sound of your own shoes hitting the ground- The joy of like a purposeful motion that is currently purpose-less – and is still occurring- the only thing there is you though- so you alone and you are walking a purposeless path- but this is like the most powerful experience- When someone is fully ready to find God they will. But it will be in God's own time and in God's own way… this Truth must be understood; God does not waste energy, ever. By bringing you to him you begin to find a sense of unshakable certainty. What this means is that you no longer possess an uncontrollable self-doubt but rather a point of Truth within you that never fades or can be disguised to those with eyes to see. God is beyond us in more ways than one and in that place of surrender we can find a more purposeful and peaceful life in which we can do so much good and can be loved all the life long. **ARCHANGEL MICHAEL BLESS US ALL. THAT ONE FOR SAFETY.**

The Archangel of Safety!

The great beatific nature of all of creation exists but isn't a Path it is certainly impossible to deny – in such words. The freedom available in it and in you is what we are all about says this author. The grace of God's showmanship is never enough it brings us all to the fakest tears possible and only polite clapping. This honesty is like a moving joint it's just a natural function- Then your mind when it is swarmed and swooned by an air of sleeping arrogance that acts as a shield against the winds of constant change that are wholly responsible for all true paths- for we aren't meant to stay walking in the mud and sand and weeds but rather meant to build paths that are to be seen and used effectively- so in that we carry on a natural expansion – the Path toward God.

The grace of Life and simply being here isn't enough it is not even qualified to be considered on any scale at all. It is not an intentional act I suppose – but can be seen more clearly as not our fault for sure! So, then we encounter the barren openness of our shared landscape with our vision and something in us shows up – also in this way it doesn't matter if it is all about some past context- but is so very relevant ultimately so. It begins to shatter the place in us that seemed so certain- but is now revealed as a stitching that was twisted and sickly- and had to end.

This moment is nothing and it is totally yours- It is so succumbed to God's holy will that is enough- I pray you are not afraid of joining your feet and eventually your soul to the path formed clearly by others in the past- for the sake of our sorrowful passion, aha. ! I pray further you recognize the aspect of yourself that is scared and don't listen to it but rather become a learner of Life not something or anything else- that is the Path TOWARD GOD.

11
KARMA

Karma is a wild, world-renowned idea. Karma seems to be prevalent in several big belief systems, which is a good indication of some kind of truth, you can look at it plainly and see for yourself. Karma is based in the soul and is designed by God to teach souls and to free the pure consciousness from its mind games. Karma is the basic principle of cause and effect that permeates our universal reality.

The way that I explain Karma is that if we are all one form, or all one soul then when we cause something to happen to another we are really causing an effect that is within some kind of closed off circle.

So, the idea is that in Buddhism we escape this by somehow, someway, releasing everything and transcending the boundaries between the finite and the infinite. But when you see things from a more realistic perspective you see that freedom is forever.

When one hand injures another hand on the same body that is injurious to the whole not just the one hand. This is the basic teaching of karma. The way of karma is a way of seeing. It is a way of perceiving and you learn much faster than without. There is something in reality called the law of conservation of energies or momentum. This rule is scientific but is also applicable to this topic of karma. When our soul begins to repeat and repeat specific lines of functioning we become entrenched and in this we find a momentum occurring.

When we stop we can begin freshly if we are lucky and courageous enough to face things anew. But this is also the case in the other way, when monks pray for several lifetimes they create positive karma!

This soul momentum is real just as karma is real but freedom is actually more real. So, with this in mind we take the pressure off our soul and find some repose in the presence of love. God is without karma for God is everything and nothing, perfect. Karma is a law created by God to conduct the universe without effort from God. Karma can be completely dropped in a moment. And when that happens ... you tell me how. Grace is powerful.

There must be something to be said about the role of the guru in this process of enlightenment and purification of past karmas, which can be a disturbing topic to imagine that your past lives have some current affect on you but if you get real Zen you find tranquil emptiness a quiet companion.

The guru can remove unpleasant karma from you if God allows it to be so.

The heart does this out of unquenchable desire to be loving and also because an enlightened heart can work miracles unseen. So, when you see that unconditional love is at work you are in the hands of the guru and of God. To me a great saint is Neem Karoli Baba *. He is a simple man with a simple plan. Love everyone. So, when we have such a guru we can trust we are headed toward a one-on-one encounter with reality, which is both objective and subjective. The Universal Truth is unconditional enlightened love.

The guru is the one who brings one's soul from darkness into its own light. We find more than we probably desire in that experience. The soul that is old enough to know God in every moment is practically enlightened and that soul's purpose is then to liberate other souls from bondage. When the heart of the soul sets its aim on God the Lord will not ignore that. Even though we may feel alone in our present lives God is a constant friend to our soul. The one soul. The All-Soul.

My one friend that I loved dearly and who shall remain nameless in this encryption said to me "If there is a soul and there is past and future lives then that means we are all each other, every other lifetime is a past or future life of our own soul."

This fact hit me hard. I saw something that I didn't see earlier. This is the wisdom of an old soul or an enlightened heart. God has so much confidence in those who have confidence in God that they can achieve literally anything. Nirvana included.

So, the great teacher Papaji taught the lesson of wisdom "Just keep quiet". His story of enlightenment is as follows: He had a yearning for God and his Truth to be in him since being a child. His most famous apprentice is Mooji. Papaji lived his life devoted to Krishna and would dance all night singing and praising God through the form of Krishna, the blue bodied being.

So, Papaji eventually encountered a knockout to his ego with Ramana Maharshi in Arunachala.

He awoke from the dream of illusory sleeping when Ramana Maharshi said the words "You have arrived." So, Papaji's teaching is simple, just keep quiet. Just keep quiet. Just .. keep .. quiet. At this moment all beings are all beings. This quiet moment. This is awareness being aware. This is the emptiness answering a prayer for liberation and sanctification. And meditation. Love is the way. The greatest healing is fully accepting Love and becoming that Love rather than anything else.

Karma is not some silly or take-it or leave-it term we can just employ like a card in our hand. It is something we can make happen or prevent but it isn't bad it is just ultimately just. It realizes itself- and we are subject to it- it is assured and the goal of life some would say is to find yourself resting upon it!

The sociological aspect is not relevant in context of our Karmic life for we can't have relationship with it as like with anything else- it is fixed within us and further in there in which there is no comings and goings made possible anymore but that this actuality of life and other souls is serious and matters and great goodness is realizable and needed across our shared world!

12
WHAT DOES IT MEAN TO BE TRULY SUCCESSFUL?

Success is a very desirable thing. It has a lot of sway and influence with people's minds and their life-long priorities. The catch is viewing success in a non-duality manner, for example instead of seeing the polarity of success versus failure to perceive it all as a worthwhile experience that is meaningful and desirable in a bigger way than a momentary success or failure mindset.

The change over from one way of experiencing life to another is crucial and is unavoidable/inevitable …my desire is to enable children and other age groups to enjoy this shift from one limited mindset to a more expanded way. I feel that instead of people being small minded forever we could become more inclusive and release our judgments that lead to repetitive and wasteful exclusive based perspectives.

So, drawing upon my own very personal experience I have had many questionable moments with others in which I have been blatantly attacked verbally and emotionally. I have seen the strength and resilience of my inner light. I have used these feather-ruffling experiences to my and the collective consciousness's greater purpose and benefit.

The majority of these select kinds of experiences are based around me being completely open and honest in front of people who may or may not have been strangers to the point of complete vulnerability and then my open heart loving throughout the intense judgments and accusations made against me and my character. Instead of seeing these experiences as unnecessary or undesirable I decided to see them as the actual necessities for my personal and soul growth. I have seen many raw Truths and have come through them a bit shaken but more well-rounded in my understanding.

I feel that being rejected from an entire small community as one of the most difficult experiences to survive and I have gone through this several times that as serious as it seems it now would make me laugh rather than fret and I would immediately question the innate intentions of their group at their core. What are they really about? I am willing to stand alone, utterly and completely. I would actually enjoy it. Complete solitude. So, for me I would say that I am serving God's purpose by revealing the truth of God's heart to those who want for it.

I see that people who are in intense emotional spaces internally (or externally) are longing for this love and sometimes the love becomes too powerful and overwhelming for them. And they end up responding violently and do everything in their egos power, which operates in small time rather than big time.

Small time is linear and is based on science and man-made measurements. Big time is God's time… souls time. The soul will return to its source eventually. The soul will return to the real guru over and over again throughout incarnations. So, from a small-minded perspective we can see these rejections as personal and devious but in a greater mind of the Lord we feel only compassion for them. From a cosmic perspective we see the entirety and in that way of perceiving we find a simple longing to help others. This is essentially what the enlightened heart is.

When one attains moksha he/she finds a sense of opening to a more simple and less rigid movement through existence as existence rather than someone struggling within the storm they become the storm and feel for everyone in their heart space. To return to the point of this installation; success is to find that awareness in which you find the inherent value in everything.

The joy in the suffering is the greatest Zen teaching.

Success is an illusion if you make it so. Maybe you would rather be empty and void, or maybe you would rather be aimless or alone. Maybe success is too much of a hassle or maybe you just feel happiness around you. And then just maybe you feel that as good enough without needing more.

One of the most urgent issues is greed. To unconsciously be motivated without a sense of reason is an obvious danger to a collective consciousness such as ours on our Earth, the cosmic Earth. We have the realistic and necessary choice to make; will we end war and provide for ourselves? We can heal humanity one good choice at a time.

~On a global scale we simply need to set clear intentions that we all wish to be happy and remove suffering!~

With this in mind we can feed, clothe, and house every single soul on the planet. To me true success is not dependent on anything. True success is beyond your circumstances and is a deep peace that is abiding and everlasting. Real success is transcendent and rather than coming from temporary experiences is beyond them and is always available. Enlightenment.

So, as we remember our innocence and surrender our pride we become elevated and buoyant rather than sullen or heavy in our souls. To have the grace to be able accept anything is a major success in this world of varied feelings and layers of feelings. When one accepts one finds the reality presents itself and worry ceases.

So, this is why I originally stated my opinion in this entry as success beyond duality, not success or not success. But that everything is for a reason and to accept that even without knowing the reason for ourself.

To be willing to disappear for the sake of Truth is a great success. I am not talking about suicide I am talking about reality. I am talking about the eternal realm. But in another manner of talking of success, to be financially successful is not that different actually, or emotionally. To be spiritually and financially successful can be compared and contrasted. The universal laws are the same throughout; as above so below. The birds of Paradise choose to land on the hand un- grasping; so, the Buddha; the awakened one who has released striving and has been kissed by the grace of the universe and also the grave. What is real prospers and what is dead remains dead. So, that is the law of attraction in a nutshell.

The one who is open receives. Money is no exception. But there are variables in existence that cannot be controlled or understood. Love is something to focus on. What we focus on begins to grow. We focus on love and we begin to generate our own unique flavor of Love. There is no greater success than to be in the arms of Love constantly, as I am. God bless you and may you find your way.

13
THE IMPORTANCE OF ADVENTURE

At some point in everyone's life they encounter the raw sensation of adventure. It may not be even an external adventure per se but adventure none-the-less. So, as any good philosopher would do, you must first define the term you are analyzing, which is known as semantics. The term we are looking at is "adventure". Adventure means a glaringly new and raw experience that may or not be of your choosing. To give creedence to ALL of history there is been so much of this and yet we see it as an overwhelmingly positive thing. Well, I guess we can say maybe it is more about our attitude in life and our demeanor towards the future as in comparison to being in opposition to anything- That is what adventure is: There is no opposition in it but it is a focusing of one's energy into themselves and a determination and excitement that is completely individual and can only be continued on by the outside world's existence- so we naturally become grateful and smiling at it- and we pick out certain goals and tasks with all kinds of seriousness or simplicities- that are woven between our inner self and our shared objective world. Thus the Importance of Adventure!

For example, I had a great adventure time when I was :

Lost in Paris for the better chunk of one day. I wasn't planning on it, and no one else I was with on this trip was planning on it, except maybe God.

I went out for a jog at 4:20 am on a clear French morning and as some may know the street layout of Paris is nothing like the grid pattern of Manhattan. It is winding and very unorganized. The Parisians I am sure are used to it like the back of their hands, but foreigners desperately need a map.

I woke up this morning and decided to join my friend and bunkmate on this jog before our day was to begin with many planned activities. God had other plans. I began the jog following after my long-legged friend and the space between kept increasing after each turn of the corner and soon I was completely alone.

As this became my new reality, being completely alone

in the lovely Paris morning I only knew one phrase; the name of my hotel and with a question mark afterwards – "hotel mercure ivry?" I only asked one person this question, a French businessman crossing the street seeming to be a bit too much in a hurry. He immediately responded "no." And continued onward.

I, at this point, had the inclination to continue searching for my hotel rather than sitting still. I learned later on that it is better to stay still in this case for future reference. I began walking in a general direction that I thought was correct and repeatedly encountered failure, thinking that the hotel must be just around the corner, the next one, must be the next one. I ended up walking, just walking. I walked for several miles, approximately 10 kilometers away from my origin. I remember walking throughout the city and seeing the faces of the women.

I remember walking, and I even remember my outfit. I was wearing exercise breeze pants and a St. Joe's T-Shirt, my high school in Buffalo, NY.

The Importance of Adventure

I was strangely fascinated with this new sense of freedom and adventure, raw emptiness. No Identification, No means of communication, no currency. Just me. I walked along for several hours and remember thinking of how enjoyable it was but what immediately ruined it or brought me down very rapidly was the fact that my parents, who were on this trip, were so worried by this time. So, my only worry was their worry. I ended up returning to the hotel eventually when I found English speaking people in some embassy station. It might have been a taxi place.

So, the lovely religious aspect of this experience was that my birth Mother in her final resort prayed with an open heart to Mother Mary* who, from her perspective, returned me home. I showed up 10 minutes later, walking up the driveway.

So, this is my adventure story among many I have had. This one is the most obvious and perhaps the most relevant for the purposes of this book. So, why did I bring this up? Why do I feel, of all the topics I could have chosen, why 'the importance of adventure'? Why?!

I would say the important aspect of real adventure time is that you are face-to-face with the stark reality. You are one with your surroundings. You are bare and the world becomes bare. You realize what is relevant very quickly. You open up if you are smart to what is occurring around you and within you and in that moment there is a symbiosis happening. Which becomes more of a Zen reality. Where there is no time for judging and only the moment, the moment, the damn moment.

And, it could be anything. It could be facing your favorite fear or it could be a rush or it could be just something you didn't plan for. But no matter what, it is guaranteed to be fresh, new, raw, and apparently necessary for your soul to grow. You learn much more viciously about yourself when you are in adventure mode. I believe the spiritual lesson available for those who are ready is facing the abyss and the unknown. The experience of being lost in any meaning of the sense is an experience of magnanimous proportions. It places an ultimate demand on the experiencer that is out of one's control. It is a very good time to surrender.

It is a very good choice to make to relax. It is a very simple moment even though we think it is different it is simple. And when we can accept the unknown we can accept anything even ourselves. We can accept the parts of us we don't like or approve of. We accept the ugliness that we hide, we accept the anger, the shame, the guilty pleasures we indulge in secret spaces. We accept it all for no reason besides that it is that way.

And then grace occurs and we open to this world anew. We find solace in the inevitable because we surrender our struggle with it. And somehow we are living in alignment with all that is. Somehow we are successful; somehow we perceive differently the cosmic wonder. Somehow we are happy and peaceful and can be-friend anyone and anything … any experience. And then … eventually … we find emptiness. And we can just breathe. And float in God's heart. Ram.

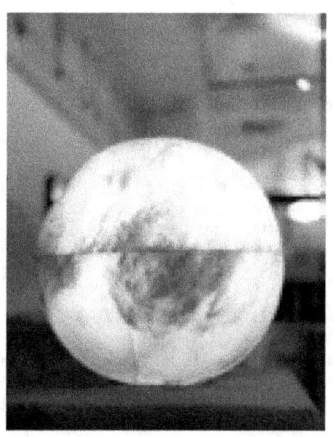

14
THE QUESTION OF MORALITY

As someone who has spent a lot of time and acquired many experiences around churchgoers I feel there are definitely some very distinct values that my friends possess and now it is time for me to reveal my own. I have done a lot of thinking on this particular topic over my life. I have tried many times to nail down the truth, morally speaking as well as in other ways. I have come to my wits end. I know this will sound ridiculous to a lot of believers but I must be honest because I do love myself and I deserve to be exactly who I am made to be, which is way awesome.

I must preface this crucial post with the truth, my truth. I believe in God. I also believe in evolution. I also believe something called cultural relativism. I believe that the most important aspect of reality is unconditional Love but instead many people feel that being right and avoiding wrong is worth our worry. I am not condoning horrible behavior that would most likely be out of alignment with your actual excitement but I am not stressing or demanding that anyone do anything in particular, including "earning" heaven or "avoiding" hell.

I feel that there is a desire to be good and sometimes there is a desire to rebel. But one must see the difference only for their own spiritual growth and for no other reason, which includes being kind to other souls and caring for them. Love is confusing sometimes because it does not diminish when we "fail" nor does it amplify when we "earn" more of it.

Love is the constant of God, Love is the eternal factor that penetrates all realities and perspectives of which there may or may not be infinite. To me it is very simple; to do good should feel good, and when you are contradicting that too much you feel un-good or unpleasant. So, when speaking to children it is important for many reasons including social survival that we are clear examples of a trustworthy character that they can rely on for guidance and who is safe to be around.

~Doing too many energetically wasteful things disturbs the equilibrium of the energy body and does not make children wish to follow or listen to you.~

These questions are very complicated when we look at them with unnecessary pressure but when we release that craving for being absolutely correct we feel relief and in that relief we come back to center, to a natural state to our actual self. To me the most genuine sense of self I can possibly have is when I am in the perfection of stillness and music and there is an effortless flow of expression that has no beginning nor end and has no other purpose but to be experienced, expressed fully, and heard, and to be felt fully. The energy of enlightenment has a real pull to it… it is God reeling you in to shore I suppose. When we tune into this we can feel the magnetism and we move quickly through self-demeaning behaviors rather than dwelling too heavily on them.

The Dalai Lama once said "Silence is sometimes the best answer."* What did he mean? I believe that in today's present age as westerners we have a lot of mental constructs that are impeding the overall joyful experience of humanity. To be silent is to be still. It is to allow everything to be everything and to allow you to be you. That is the meaning of being still and there is divinity in that.

So, what can we say about morality now if there is just silence? But, I must say the inclination I have towards exposing the Truth as I believe I am in the process of doing right now is …interesting.

Why would I need to do this or that? If I somehow was always taken care of and I didn't need to stress over anything would I still do anything at all? The answer is at this moment, yes. I could be still but something deeper stirs me and convinces me to write on, to sing on, to perform, to learn, to grow, to heal, to suffer, to blossom further, and to teach. All in the name of God's Love and a desire to be free. So, instead of boringly stating many platitudes of old I decided to tell the truth, my truth. There is not always going to be a distinct right or wrong! You must learn that and realize that your happiness is not controlled by the universe or some collection of good merits. There is a great relief and heart opening and healing in that truth because that is the perspective of unconditional Love. So, I would like to attempt to answer this question: what is the ultimate good? To me goodness if it is of any relevance to us is inherent to us from our birth. It cannot be taught then. It has to be present in our experience for it to be real.

The real good is not manufactured, it is an attribute of God in heaven. Real good-natured beings have no reason to be good besides for its own pleasure and sake. The main and distinct differences if you care to know them between positive and negative energy is as follows: negative energy segregates, positive energy includes/unifies. But, this can become very different when we see things in absolutes.

Subjective and objective realities can all meet in the heart space and somehow can be resolved for the greater benefit of the cosmic self; God, in all its glory.

So, seeing morality from a dualistic perspective we see the extremes of dark and light rather than the spectrum of it all. Darkness is an illusion of no free will and light is a revelation of pure choice. Light is information dark is misinformation. Emptiness is simply a break from both. To wrap up this section we should have some clarity; Much of the times when we seek to do "good" and seek to stop "bad" we are really just seeking safety, acceptance, and belonging. Something that I have learned from my stay in the monastery is the law of unconditional acceptance. There is a quality of God that is a function of unconditional love that is unconditional acceptance once safety is found and maintained.

So, for example in the monastery you have all your basic needs met being food, shelter, clothing, warmth in the winter and cool in the summer, and a beautiful sense of community as well as opportunity for growth. Now after this is the case there becomes this amazing complete feeling of acceptance, the entirety of "you" becomes accepted by these other monks, who are acting as extensions of source (God), the good and the bad, the happy and the sad, the violent and the depressed, the joyful and the ecstatic, all of this is accepted.

This is the power of Love it can and will change your life for it gave birth to you and will watch as you breathe for the last time on this earth realm; who knows what happens next? Does it matter when you are one with Love in its essence in its entirety, which is God? Be kind, do not cause harm but if you must do it with your heart and realize that all pain is an aspect of you in need of true love and healing; all the evil that exists also exists within God's heart and is surrounded with the reality of heavenly goodness. God bless you with clarity and insight. Amen.

It is Dr. Joe Vertino :)

15
THE POWER OF BEING WEIRD

We have all been there, I would hope. Being the one who is supremely different. We walk different, we talk different and we even FEEL different. So, what is the definition of weird?

Weird: the absence of a state of normal besides one you make for yourself. So, with this new definition we can refresh our soul and hopefully take some solace in that new perspective. The "normal" might be wrong... we should consider that! So, when we decide to deviate from that norm we move into our own heart.

This is why my writings are titled as such "my own religion" because I would rather be weird than normal and I want to make that obvious. I believe that the desire for true and lasting freedom is synonymous with weirdhood. The willingness or lack of aversion to this frequency streamlines the individual being into a lifestyle of pure excellence. So, the pros and cons of weirdhood:

The benefits are as follows:

1. You are free and you are released from unnecessary societal pressure and/or concern.

2. You make your own way. This means you do not have to follow anyone and that you have all that is necessary for your life inside of you roaring for your acceptance and attention and application.

3. You become an inspiration to others. You, just by being you, begin to shelter people's souls who are at odds with their current existence and you offer them hope for a new day, a new experience and a new lifestyle. What an honorable way to live and love. You lead.

I guess to be fair I will list some possible cons:

1. You may be judged, a lot. The people that are being severely challenged by your awesomeness and courage unconsciously decide to try to upset you. It is only a minor setback and you may inspire them to change.

2. You have to become okay with being alone. This is the challenge for you to fall in love with yourself and to do it fully and completely, no exceptions.

3. The willingness to move into the unknown. A lot of people fear this part because the abyss is unknown and do you even really know yourself? Then why judge the unknown, you ARE the unknown as well.

So, now that we have a beautiful comprehensive list of the experience and choice of weird-hood we can begin to consider lovingly our own life and times. Are we weird? Are we willing to be more weird? Are we willing to let go of our disillusions of the past about what "weird" meant to us? I hope so. So, the importance of this post is to empower individuals in a society such as this. To move forward in a way that is healthy, safe, but also joyful, creative, and nourishing to our mind and the soul within us. I am weird. I hope you can find your own capacity to find the real you, whom I love dearly.

So, the more we are accountable for Ourself and gain maturity we are allowing the power we actually do always possess to be growing- with the waters of Truth rather than the fires of illusion to dawn another bright sunny day- like when it is bright outside but the darkness shines forth and we feel it alone in our enclosure and yet an eternal soul. The grace that is seriously real that you don't even have to sincerely follow in church it follows you like a child who is born of your wife and needs your attention seemingly all the time, or perhaps just on saturday... This holy seriousness is making itself known to us THE DENIAL OF US BEING WEIRD - which can never logically be its power.

Conclusion:
The general assembly of this great soul you and its incarnations is present and staring it down - this whole occasion I lay before your holy and-known-in-me presence - right here right now- it shines , shines, forth. I beckon you onward to Nirvana- Trust is next. This day can wait. So, what is it? THE POWER OF BEING WEIRD OF COURSE. May we not need too much recourse to these wise words in the form of a book, may we not, may we stop and feel and realize and change now... gently gently. May we perceive simply and lovingly our own gaze - surrender may it come and not be thwarted at all, no attempt. may this angel you send , Lord, come to give some gentle but purposeful tap to send us forth a push of your wind dear mother father God- may we steal away to you for it is weird.

We are in the mountains says some folk and across our reckless but laughing journey in foreign lands aplenty before unseen- an exciting journey but weird to mine eyes henceforth. This one seer is mine. I am embellished with both the jewel of this foreign land, my own homes, and this go between the jewel of my mind of it all- and I must give credit where credit is do - all this in the name of the Power of Being Weird- nowhere to foresake or fetch without it in my wings whether I sit or flutter further on ... and on. Down the road til the road is no more. And yet and like a sword of folded steel it sits inside my belly with its memory - deep in my soul forever- as under a murderers touch- I go to Nirvana with my proud self in tact - and honored to have been made apparently in the image of our creator- and in my power I stand and fall WEIRD upon the dear and deer eaten Earth and grass and beg and moan already for another lifetime to witness the seeping in our your truest vine and drink the wisdom through courageous thought it groans a new.

So know you know me ? ... it said

I love you regardless.

Angel Blessings

This design is called THE FLOWER OF LIFE

16
WHAT IS LOVE, REALLY?

Love, in its essence, is just a word. So, when you see that love is somehow everything, just like God, it can be different to try to understand and to define. Love to me is like an energy cloud that sometimes just floats there in your face. It doesn't necessarily do anything in particular but it just makes you feel special.

You are Love. Everything inside of you is love. That is why we are so confused because we are searching and searching for something else. You are "the something else." You are the answer to your own questions.

I would always answer my own questions thinking that God was answering them for me and speaking through my mouth into my own ears. Having an unlimited amount of conversation with the creator of all is a unique experience of unconditional love.

So, to me love is also Samadhi. Samadhi is an ancient Sanskrit word where in the consciousness of a person transcends the mundane and moves into an expanded awareness in which the mind becomes very free and opens. But this experience is real and then we return into our forms and incorporate this enlightenment experience or satori into our daily lives.

Love could be seen as play when someone is enjoying something so much that they forget their reason for starting and are simply in the do-er-ship of it all (a.k.a doing something for the sake of it.) Love to me is deep rest. When I hear the Zen proverb: "when you are hungry; eat. When you are tired; rest." You can understand this.

The reason this is important to me is that love can be simple. Love is adoration and a reckoning within oneself. Have you ever felt the beauty of an image and it made you vibrate deep inside? That is Love. There is a visceral experience of Love.

Love is something that is beyond us but is also the experience we are having. Love in that sense is the most humbling of all experiences. To be so completely present is also love. At therapy earlier this week my counselor was discussing Fred Rogers *, "Mr. Roger's Neighborhood"... and he said that Mr. Rogers was disrespected heavily in his hometown of Pittsburgh, Pennsylvania because of his effeminate nature and the men of that region were more machismo.

This disrespect continued into his success with his television broadcast, but he noticed that the people who poked fun at him were coming to him for assistance when he was alone. He was a great man and this is proof. The people that would make fun of him would later come to confide in him and all he would do is listen with an open heart. This is Love in its simplest form.

Love is something that is direct and pure. This is healing to us because of all the chaos of our history. When we encounter real love we begin to heal because we release our inner resistance. The real love of a trusted being is consistent even though moods change. For example, the guru and saints of ages past would have many disciples sit by them and they would follow them to the best of their ability. These wise people know how to love fully and completely, including all that is.

The people would sense that in their heart and the spiritual journey continued on but that Love is eternal. Instead of trying to make things into something else when there is this surprise of acceptance you can see how the person receives this real love right away like good medicine. How marvelous indeed.

What I am learning is how can I expect others to surrender to the love of God when I still sometimes seem to struggle against it too? ; humility. I guess I will quote one of my favorite people of all time, a mother Priorus. * She said "God gives us pain so we remain humble." I believe we were discussing something in my life and she said that to me. There is a love that is complete and cherished in the heart of a woman like her, like Jesus's mom.

She always makes me cry. I've had dreams with her and there is such an acceptance and love with her that is somehow beyond right and wrong. I've even felt sexually attracted to Mother Mary* and have expressed it, mhm. I feel that is all I could do with my energy so why not give it to God!? I feel that there is a deep peace in real love but the only thing is you can never fake Love. Even the person with small intelligence will know you are faking.

The supreme being Babaji * visits those yogis who sit up in all hours of the night in the Himalayas of India. This is Love that is purified and focused on the divinity and enlightenment of God.

To me Love is found in the dance of opposites as well. For example, the yin yang is Love, it shows the unity that is evidence of oneness between all pairs. Male and female dance inside and around each other to procreate. The creation process is a wondrous event that God created for us to enjoy and suffer through. We all know the pains of childbirth and did you know that when Lions have intercourse the male lion scrapes the inside of the female lioness and this causes her to scream?

The joy and the suffering, the harmony and the discord, the ecstasy and the agony. Love is what abides. There is a great female guru who can be found on youtube and all over the internet, she goes by Gangaji *. She has white silvery hair and a beautiful sharp smile and she has such a blunt way of loving her students that is very pleasing. The reason I bring her up is because she has a talk on youtube that was titled "The heart can bear it all." VIDEO IN LOG OF MEDIA- *

She is right. And I have often thought back on that title especially when bearing pain even if it isn't my own pain. But the true heart doesn't even know or care whose pain it is all the heart, the one heart, so how can there be others? Then how could there be others pain when there is only one God, one heart, one consciousness, one criminal and one victim, yes. Saying yes, to the pain, allowing the insufferable to be experienced. Mother Mary bore pain when seeing Jesus * on the crucifix for no reason but to prove to the people that Love is willing to suffer and die for its own sake. Love is beyond pain and pleasure this is real Love to me.

17
GRACE: WHAT IS IT, WHY IS IT RELEVANT?

Grace is something God given and underserved by my definition. I have first hand experience with grace and that qualifies me to some degree to teach and write about this topic. I feel that when someone already is in a state of grace the grace then becomes clearer to his or her spiritual eyes and then it grows in intensity and frequency. The importance of grace is that it is a direct proof of God's love and apparent intervention. Grace is relevant to all beings because it is beyond our grasp yet it is something that affects us deeply. For some reason Mother Mary, the mother of Jesus, comes to my mind in this case- again as in the last chapter.

I believe that could be because of the "Hail Mary" prayer… "Hail, Mary, full of grace the Lord is with thee…" It says she is full of grace. So, I would say we could focus on her for this entry. What does it mean to be full of

God's power and grace on a constant basis? I would say that since I am very close with Mother Mary that my opinion has merit. I believe Mother Mary is full of God's grace but how could we know what that perspective is? Is it even possible for us to imagine that? I would say that our imagination is very powerful and we may be tapping into the reality of grace through our minds imagining.

So, why is this relevant to us in this lifetime?

I believe God's inherent value and grace is sometimes God's best means of communication. Grace is a very similar vibration to the essence and energies of prayer. I guess the greatest gift of grace is true wisdom. This is daunting because it means all that is not real will perish. So, this is essentially the point of the spiritual journey. There is a spiritual exercise called "neti, neti" which translates from the ancient language of Sanskrit as "not this, nor that". So, what this is used for is the removal of that which is a distraction to the ultimate reality- pure aware being.

So, to me being full of something first requires that container to be empty. So, this spiritual practice is designed to eliminate the false. But, once this is the case you could say that grace remains, and grace is just the overflowing, unconditional, reckless love of God. So, what is the point of it all then? Is it just to move from falsehood to clarity or to be like God? To be full of grace to the point where you cannot stop the love and wisdom from filling those around you? Is it moving from darkness into Lightness? Perhaps that's why they call it En-Light-enment. So, we could go the distance and say what really is real? What remains after death dawns? The body becomes the earth, the thoughts based in the corporeal mind cease with the body, I assume.

The essence remains, is that God? Is that the soul? So, when we die we live? I have heard it said that to die to our small self is to live as the big self. So, to give in to the greater self of God is to truly live, this means for us that we move eventually into that reality either gracefully or violently. So, returning to grace, which is what I wish for you. Gracefully, we can surrender our struggle with all just by being perfectly in oneness with the creator energies that are ever around you, even now, especially now. Feel that, Christos. Feel the Buddha field. Feel the salve, the salvation, the complete inevitable surrender into the nothingness of God's heart and complete presence. No more fearing, nothing more but what is real!

Grace abides just as Love does. Grace is the hand of God. Love is the essence and opening up. When we finally allow our eyes to rest on God we combine our individual energy with the cosmic awareness of flawless reality. What does it matter to us if we are gracious? It matters to me, for sure. I see the Lord of Love as its own purpose and that is good enough for me because Love never dies, loses, or bores. It is always fresh and exciting! Grace is this book. Grace is the mind I was given and the heart I reside in. Grace is perfect as you are perfect. Grace is the overabundance of perfection. To be truly "full of Grace" is to be absent from selfhood and to move as spirit and you are one being. That is enough words on something that must be experienced personally to be fully comprehended. Amen.

Teal Swan the Spiritual Catalyst and her divine Art

18
WHAT IS SOUL -LOVE?

First, as always, is semantics. Definition of the soul:
The collection of experiences flooding and coalescing with every lifetime (incarnation) that is accessible through the energy body and chakra system. This is an ancient concept throughout human history. The chakras are points of awareness that belong to and provide access to the soul's lens. Then as we attune our chakras to the soul we begin to develop our own unique perspective on God. Then Love is something that we already know. So, Soul-love is a beautiful experience that is completely unseen. The soul as it is difficult to find but once you attune your mind to it you can see it very clearly and obviously. It can even become overbearing. And the next quality of the soul is its lack of judgment and its amazing ability to know our innermost self. So, when we allow this part of ourselves to receive and give love, that is what is known as soul-love.

There is an intimacy that is possible within and throughout the soul reality. The soul is designed to experience. It has lived for a very long time and when we move from our soul realm into a reality of oneness we experience more as God and less as something individual. So, the difficulty the ego has with the soul is because it doesn't play by our rules. In fact, sometimes it will willfully mess our plans up and go against our "rules". So, after this life is over your soul remains and at some point the pure awareness is more real, for example the soul is transcended and can be used as a moving place to move into God. And then God is what remains.

Back to the point of this excerpt… soul Love is when there is a sense of oneness. A lot of the time throughout my day I find myself saying the word "Anahata"*; this is the Sanskrit word for Heart. There is a gradient to the soul- moving from darkness into light. There is a spectrum to it.

So, this is something I wanted to tell you to help you develop an understanding of what is considered Soul-Love. The belief I have on this is that what makes someone an old soul is that they have acquired a lot of experience.

What makes someone a teaching soul is that they used their incarnation time to prosper, BUT I feel it is very important to know that wisdom is only useful if it helps other souls.

What would it be like for someone or something to know you so deeply that you have no hope of hiding anything? This is something people think would be called intimacy but it can be unpleasant when there is a misunderstanding or a sense of judgment. So, something that I am working on with my own soul relationship is learning to fully Love my soul for all that it is, without trying to make it better or different.

So, something I am familiar with is the label of being a "good" soul. What does this mean and why is it relevant? I would say it is important to be a good soul because it means that you have found a sense of groove with existence; God is close to you and you to that; or a sense of Oneness. And eventually you release the resistance you have clutched for a while when you surrender into God's Love as it is. You find the joy and grace of a deep sense of belonging to that which is infinite called God. So, for example I just enjoy writing about this even though a lot of what I say comes to the same point.

Why do the Buddhist's believe there is an absence of a Soul? They rather would perceive the soul as a flame that moves from one candlewick to another one. This serves a purpose to eliminate excess stress of the mind when meditating. If you are trying to quiet the mind contemplating too much will be an issue for them I suppose.

I believe that Love is the only energy that truly quiets the crying baby of the mind and that has nothing to do with the existence of or absence of a soul. But, continuing on with that line of thinking is that the mind is not a pest it is a boon. This shift is important because then we stop trying to destroy our mind as if it is an enemy. But when we can perceive the mind we see that there is awareness that is perpetual. We can see the grace in this statement and revelation of reality. Our reality may be considerably simpler than escaping suffering; it may be even grander; there is a clue here that I will explain in detail. The clue is this: you ARE awareness. And your mind is an experience that you are having as awareness! I Hope that makes it clear for you.

The process of Soul-Love can be spontaneous OR it can take place over a long time. But when it is present it is overwhelming and undeniable and very recognizable. What happens is that you feel understood, plainly.

You feel that who you are beyond right and wrong is loved deeply, this is the point of Soul-Love. To establish a connection with one unique drop of God with another one, one soul to another soul. The reason this is deserving of its own excerpt is because it is universal. We can find a deep sense of vulnerability and safety within this relationship, we can find some beautiful healing with this because we need to feel validated in all our experiences and the soul when it is admired properly can heal.

Soul-Love can also be felt more consistently between a student and his/her teacher. This is very important to me. I feel that the knowledge of one soul moving another soul towards God is of immense value and purpose on this planet at this time. I feel that is the basic real Guru relationship. The true guru is a doorway to the divine vast sky. I understand the intricacies and subtleties of love as it unravels our disguises and establishes with our trust and permission new ones based on God's love and not our own love of self. This is the grace of the guru at play in our soul bringing us into a divine radiance to better serve the Lord who liberates us all.

I thought of two very powerful books but in particular a style of writing that is; basically called "meditations."

Thomas Merton has at least one that I know of and also, Sir Thomas Moore maybe I know David Stendl-Raast a strong monk also has a book in that style– I am mentioning them in context of this chapter because it is a deep seated need, desire, craving for what "Soul-Love" is and it is more important that we fulfill that than it is that we appease the other things in our life that may only MAYBE lead to Soul-Love. So how we accomplish this is by communing with that which gives rise to all the possible personalities we can ever recognize. And since we deserve to fully resonate (with our soul wide open) we are acknowledging and giving in to this greatest desire rather than giving in to hate for others by way of not helping us resonate with this sacred thing called Soul-Love with in an external relationship and then also inevitably surrendering to the experience of despair that comes after the denial-based choices. So- it is appropriate for you to immediately allow this possibility into your life, that's all. This possibility that you can have a full and deep experience without the rug being pulled out from under your newly aclimitized ankles… and as you live you can recognize, again, that great way that allows for more of your true self to come about which is here and now UNKNOWN and is needed by God; come on baby!

19
THE THREE JEWELS

In the ancient spiritual lifestyle known as Buddh-ism there is a foundation laid known as the three jewels, you may see these jewels now in your imagination; your mind's eye.

The first jewel: The Buddha
This is the center point on which all of the prayer wheels revolve. In Tibetan culture the concept of revolution is very popular, they have golden prayer wheels that are made of solid metal and are spun as people move by them. Also, they have microcosmic representations of these for the hands... some may call them Vajra, but the one I am mentioning specifically here is the spinning cylinder of prayer used during meditation or mantric practice.

The Buddha is the cosmic SunLight, the sun itself, the things of movement move, the nature of The Buddha is a bit different, it enters this world and adheres to it with great loving attentiveness. We are sometimes feeling like we are spinning in the void, when we are ready we enter the void As this Buddha. The Buddha is the goal of enlightenement that doesn't come and go- it doesn't really move- it brings souls towards though and shines without any agenda and sometimes apparent reason. It demands your Spiritual attention even when you don't know anything about Spirituality in this very lifetime. It is perpetually found and is also a saving grace and you may find yourself developing a relationship with it but and when other relationships are not there and they come and go like the rain and sometimes not so pleasant. And this fateful meeting will be in eternity forever. The first jewel of THE BUDDHA is the goal of enlightenment that doesn't disappear. It shines and is the root of true awakening. This swerving of all these things in the worlds can stop. And we see just the Buddha, and you are having a NEW experience in a new way without any of those things shifting just at all- and you swerve less. You and only you between yourself and eternity this first jewel. Amen.

The 2nd Jewel; The Dharma

(Our) Dharma is the practice we sustain throughout our lifetime and it has a specific purpose. Some say it is the most potent medicine for our existence. When we can see through the eyes of the soul we can see the Yogi as the constant dharmic. What this means is they are simply dealing with their own existence in comparison or recognition of divinity, the Buddha Sun. They practice Yoga for this lifetime as a commitment and they see the resolution of misused energies.

The idea of a devoted practice is to be awake even when the sun has set and the moon is there now. For example, it has been said that when our body sleeps the "mind" stays awake and alive in its own sameness with all that is, the Buddha mind. So, as we awaken in the morning can we remain in our mind that is Buddha? This is my take on Dharma or spiritual ritualism/practice.

Furthermore, it takes great discipline and faith to first find our dharma and to commit to it with the strength of our soul. THE DHARMA is the purpose driven life of God that reveals itself to all souls- as we properly employ our free will everyday and begin to shine like THE BUDDHA (see above*). The dharma can be so commonplace or so grand in context of the entire world we are in externally but the shifting sands of the mind do not need our attention nor do we need to prove anything in combination with completing DHARMA ALONE. It is ever available and is possessive in a poetic or mystical way- It is CERTAINLY INCLUSIVE and never can be possible for it to increase suffering; inherently. It has no personhood but it can feel as if we are in a relationship with- further the 5 Reiki Principles- the third Reiki Principle is "Just for today... I will do my work honestly"... *

The Dharma is that ONE THING we must attune ourself to- It is like the biggest loving bubble that we cannot escape- it is powerful and is constantly a connecting force for us into the true power that pervades all creation- and ultimately it is forever our choice; Dharma. It enables Faith and all goodness by its simple and eternal way- It shows and brings us further into Light always- It is appropriate of us all to design our shared world in context of its needed promotion for all souls. The frequency of the Truth is all pervasive but that is not something we can take from and include though is it "real"... The only way Dharma exists is when we as people choose it- the point of wisdom is to indicate to us all where in lies our personal DHARMA.

The calling is clearly present but we as individuals are in this constant struggle perhaps without including DHARMA into our life. The swelling of the heart occurs through this simple jewel /refuge. And we are meant to be truly proud.

The third jewel; The Sangha:

The community of God centered individuals, the definition or personal perspective ON God is not so important to the sangha, but the energy of Loving awareness is of utmost importance, a true modern day spiritual community should not be held back in any way especially by belief systems orbiting the minds of the members. When we find the resolve to enter a sangha fully and completely we should feel an immense sense of relief and resolve. The reason for this is because actual reality is now being consciously attended to as opposed to survival mode alone, this shift causes great joy.

If you must know what I mean, the monastery is not to lock us in it but is rather to lock the illusion away, more clearly stated; the physical distractions of 3rd dimensional life (Ram ram). And then we can fully face our own inner distractions with real safety and perseverance and see with the mind's eye an all encompassing actuality of Love and freedom to be the Love we inevitably discover. The energies of masculine and feminine divinity find their own way into the heart when we set aside the unconscious fears as Zen master Rama * demonstrated (supremely recommended). He has a video, a zen tape, in which he discusses this balance of our inner man and inner woman.

Link to a *video* in LOG OF MEDIA !

The culmination of these three jewels manifests in a higher dimensional reality, or a more joyful lifestyle. Happy Enlightenment!

Sangha just as mentioned above for the second one- we are meant to be proud and also to be relaxed. So, this requires foundation! Sangha is the community that has enough knowledge to remain in and of a helpful place (to and for all). The Sangha is a place in which the precious can emerge- the remedial can fall away- meaning the lesser parts. As a Reiki master we know this is of utmost important. The manner in which we commune is another experience of our dear soul and it carries weight- and we are PURIFYING our self when we dive into this consciously and politely. The FULLNESS OF INDIVIDUALITY is becoming of all and is accessible in the divine Sangha- which is outside of our control and our own personal potentials; unlike our dharma. It is obvious to me that the Sangha should be a common place around our shared world, kind of like a hug, that we get to flow through in our daily lives- like fish who require a tank that's kept to live on- like someone who has to cut the wild grass. We deserve to be truly happy and not suffer needlessly – and since we have the innate aspect of self-exploration in us a people we are called to live in conscious community that is foundationally aware- and exciting on a personal level.

I have a book called "The Reform of the Education System" and an idea called "Opportunities for Growth" that enables this … please look into it. Link to book and information: If you click this link and go to the bottom right you will see it there: link in LOG OF MEDIA*

(Ctrl+click to follow link)

Thee "Opportunites for Growth" have to do with my great vision for all thee Earth and how pleasing to expansion and progress our use of our resources and technology can be- collectively. I see it as the developing human is exposed to our shared world and grows in actual information and appreciation and then they are able to eventually take a more active stance as the individuation process occurs and the Truth dawns of their own personal preferences and agenda for their very lifetime is priority. We can then see how providing all these relevant "Opportunities for Growth" around the world (why not?) are so important.

If we are going to have airplanes and computers we have to engage with our humanness first and see what it is that we are attempting to achieve and what is actually the case and then what can be done to permanently reform our ways- because to me this is that one thing that needs to be solidly fixed in place and made foundational- for it is for everyone's benefit and use so to speak- generations into the future. I would love to collaborate with anyone about any of this and implement and/or counsel, advise, or optimize anything around this worldwide. And I am so glad for any and all of those things that are already in place. This is basically just a commonsense goal and foundational presence we can accomplish and instill!

The wording of it being "Opportunities for Growth" is appropriate in context of the bill of rights, thee ammendments, the constitution, and all of us being lead and founded on civility and/or government- to the point of all of them. This is what they are about and what our current systems already in place are aiming for everyday, of course some sectors or organizations are more or less involved or focused specifically but ALL of them would be glad to have thee "Opportunities for growth" Center/hubs set up around the world as divine aspects of human development! And I feel that it is appropriate, further, to have Right to Growth" in direct and clear support of the "OFG" to be made available within the Bill of Rights and ammendments as an addition to it- that would be globally successful and obviously complimentary foundationally.

20
NATURE, AND ITS HEALING ATTRIBUTES

This present topic is very dear to my heart the reason for that is because I have a deep love for Gaia the Earth. I feel that there is a simple yet powerful energy that IS mother Earth. I believe that there are some very off views about the Earth and its perfection. I feel that the divinity of Mother Earth is very obvious to me but it seems to be very hidden to others. I feel that Earth must be healed and we must also be healed. The way to do this is a real Loving relationship. Drunvalo Melchizedek* designed a very clear and simple meditation or visualization for this purpose. The meditation enables us to perceive from the heart rather than so much polarity. The idea is that the Earth loves us all in a very pure and sweet way. The Earth needs our love as we need hers, so what we do is we use our third eye imagination to empower ourselves and the planet we live on. The process is as such; we imagine all of our love for Gaia filling up our heart chakras and then as this grows and overflows we allow it to descend into the Earth all the way into the center of it. Then we wait for her to send her love for us back and we receive it happily into our heart and everywhere else. We then sit with this new refreshed and ancient relationship. We move from an ego mindset into a collective understanding. Here is the link for that, there are many videos tis one; VIDEO LOG OF MEDIA *

To continue this we do the same meditation with the cosmic bodies. So, in the Native American tradition they call it connecting the divine child in the heart with Mother Earth and with Father Sky… an ancient technique used for centering and healing purposes.

The next section of this meditation focuses on the love for the cosmos in the heart and as it glows the love is sent out the top of the spine into the galaxies … we wait and then receive the love in return and we integrate that consciously. We then rest in this completion process of a supreme Love. So, for people to find a new passionate connection with all that is you can consciously focus your love rays upon our Earth Mother. You can find a lot of security, safety, and strength that is very difficult to replicate without a real and benevolent connection with Earth.

There is a very unassuming humility with Earth vibrations. We can find a healing sense of unconditional acceptance that is unique to a society in which there is so much strife. So, to allow the humanness of who you are to be accepted and eventually fully embraced and empowered rather than shamed is a great feeling!

So, for me continuing on with Drunvalo Melchizedek in his book "The Serpent of Light"* he participates with the Lord to move the Kundalini energy (the serpent of light) of the mother Earth into its new place for the next 25-26,000 years. It is a move from Tibet into its new dwelling and purposeful place of South America, specifically Peru.

The reason I brought this up is because Drunvalo worked with the indigenous tribes all over the Earth who are constantly connected with her and they understand her. This is where the modern day man/woman needs to return to a simpler way of perception in order to move into a new dimensional reality of unconditional love, light, and liberation from limitation.

There was once a nun named Hildegaard von Bingen*; she was wondrous and would come to author a book about herbology and also was responsible for very special music. So, in context of this chapter being "nature, and its healing attributes" The monks and nuns of our Earth are so precious. They have a design! Meaning the role is very clear that they are spending this lifetime in! I am designed also and mine is providing such understanding- not all the monks and nuns can or need to do that- but I do and I will! I feel it is very appropriate use this nuns lifetime and fitting into that role as a good example for this chapter! Music enables us to more fully connect to thee Earth in the sense that we are meant to be joyful on it. And that us being connected to thee Earth even in stillnesses encourages us to produce music…. In that sense there is like a cool relationship oscillating around us; humanity, with the Earth and music.

It is like an ever repeating or unfolding circumstance- that enables more beauty to be understood and experienced! It is like a lineage of love that is pure ecstacy that I was so enamored by during my younger yet adult years I would experience in my choice of music- I would listen to the chanticles of Hidegaard von Bingen and recall very deeply in communion in my soul. I am so proud to know the Lord and to partake in the Lord's holy inspiration that brings more and more souls unto him or her! This is made possible through the efforts of such figures as her; Hildegaard! I of course have made my own music (as well my own religion, haha) Link for Dr. Joe Vertino's music: * and then also here is Hildegaard von Bingen's link for her music : LOG OF MEDIA *

So, for me the real importance of the Earth is its openness towards me always.

No matter how upset I am or how fearful or how angry or however uplifted or ascended I feel Earth is always a welcome vibration and it is stable. It is something that can change us very deeply because it is the commonality of all peoples, we are all connected through our feet. So, the ability to begin to channel our pure animal spirit we move into alignment with God very quickly. But this can be very powerful and a big shift from a fake or counterfeit manner of life to a very raw one.

The importance I feel towards the Earth is its absolute beauty that is very unassuming and does not try to impress anyone which to me is a lesson that young women can learn from her; humility and self- knowledge. It is always more attractive to be pure than to be false. The reason I see beauty in women is because they are vibrating in love and nothing else. This is the way it should be. Beauty is designed by the Lord for a specific purpose; so we can stop questioning things so heavily. And the grace I pray for right now is that people can trust in the sheer perfection of God's creation for humanity and release the unnecessary waste of energy and mind power. The Earth is something that is like self-maintained and is in that way a constant provision for us and enabling us to experience life on it all the time. We can have a better life in that perspective; for example when are children are being raised if they come to know that fact that the Earth is a self-sustaining natural fact of the cosmos they would not feel so anxious generally- but there would be a more openness in return to thee earth as I feel from it also- That there is no reason to hide from God's creation and this relationship you develop throughout your life with thee Earth becomes one of holiness, rather than anything else.

The practice of meditation that you encourage in this life is made more transcendent with the lack of denial but rather openness and by way of Logic we could say we are always on the earth, so this becomes more obvious to us and as we grow older we resonate with it and sometimes only it. All of that is healing because even to the soul in moments where we are wounded or confused any of those things the remedy is simply being open and these difficulties that we have inside of our soul, as we think of Mother Mary* who is known for untying the knots of our souls we are here by removing the obstacles to our own souls healing by encouraging an openness all lifelong- which we can say comes about by listening to such words here- rationally.

To me the great beings of the Earth are forest dwelling shamans who know things. They know things that we wouldn't be able to understand. Those beings are in perfect harmony with nature and they find a transcendent experience that is a kin to enlightenment but the difference is that it is not found through rigorous self- exertion but is a natural process and occurrence. So, back to God we find the balance of life and death in the heart of the shaman.

The shaman moves through opposites rather than being limited by them, which we are still stuck on, sadly and desperately. We can seek these people out but it will only work if we are genuine and move into our heart first and then we create the future from the heart, working with it always, never betraying it and always seeing the divine 'everything and nothing' in the little things.

The reality of the Earth is that she is not simple she is not dead she is not dumb, she is a divine being that is actually a future incarnation of a soul. Mother Earth is a conscious being that you can directly talk to. Mother Earth is the ultimate comforter. Earth finds the root of our suffering and can relieve the pressure and can replace the old ways with new ways and we find a lasting power in her Heart of love.

The great power of Love is described with Maharaji, the incarnation of the Hindu God Hanuman, the Monkey Man, thee constant servant. Neem Karoli Baba would answer his students and say to them when they ask about enlightenment and kundalini rising he would say to "Feed people and Serve People." This is the point and the power that the Earth is not something we have to move beyond, it IS the beyond as it is. The Earth is a microcosm of our great reality; the macrocosm to some degree.

I pray you feel the heartbeat of the Earth.

>	VIDEO LOG OF MEDIA; Instagram video by thee author "Connecting to the Earth" *

The human hand is a good symbol for when in pain.

21
PAIN

A human hand is not the worst thing to see in context of this very plain and obvious topic to learn from a Master Healer about. We all wish this topic was not so relevant generally. By definition pain is such a thing that it is stuck it stays there and is uncomfortable- and it seems easy to assert that the most urgent and appropriate course of action in response to it is just STOPPING. Then in that place you know you are not causing any to occur and couldn't be causing more pain personally. We must understand how important this passage is to better put our mind's in the right perspective. Since pain is something that certainly already has occurred we are inevitably the experiencer of it and would guaranteed develop an opinion of it- so let this writing be what your opinion is, what you end up believing forever about your pain! So, it is very good to use and continue using the rational mind when true pain happens because to eventually heal we must be able to allow the complete experience and to remain centered as functional as an individual that we can be we must choose to exercise some alertness in recognition of our personal pain, never anyone or anything else's pain though – which is what maturity entails. Then the aspect of ourself which is helpless and sufferous is allowed to no longer be denied and the experience at hand is had as fully as is relevant and accessible- all of this is wisdom in context of Pain. As a Reiki Master I am in awe of the infinite ability and potential of this simple and powerful modality. It is widely misunderstood and I am here to show you your own divinity, as I see it, is Rei-Ki. I have come to find my own heaven in the lifestyle of practicing Reiki, it has taught me honor and diligence and the true grit I have within to be here with you now and to bless you and heal you whether you know me or not.

We have all been blessed fiercely with real pain in this life on this planet. So, I would like to heal all of it somehow. I pray these words can fill you with a wise love. I thank you, Lord for creating in me a clean heart to better do your work and will, amen.

It is so appropriate to pray before you all humanity about just dealing with Pain- that it ends up being the only thing I can do and makes it even more clear to me what God really is and his intentions with me especially… for your benefit.

In our current affair as our shared world we have developed in such a miraculous manner we call Psychology- the scientific and self -loving way which translates as consistent help with just conversation and clear communication. Pain is very much encouraged to be discussed openly and this embrace of self is put at the height of our awareness and wins out over our unconscious will to (self) harm in anyway. What a great collective decision to manifest this. You do not have to be a genius or fit in to experience the relief of choosing to for yourself to help yourself, it's simple. And pain also does not have to be the focus or anticipated which is extremely beneficial generally for life's enjoyment but also you are more routine in proper use of free will naturally and are able to not have a perverse viewpoint on life or hopefully anything at all.

We can understand that causing pain does sometimes result in this manner of experience. So, we can understand that making choices is great having senses to experience life is great and that you in your capacities are not an enemy or are wrong.

And that Pain is simply part of that whole thing and that whole thing is always greater so to speak than the pain, and the true and lasting context of it all is our soul, which craves experience and relationships and to grow in wisdom and to heal and attain enlightenment. Pain is not a necessity but the ability to experience it is. And we must accept that our shared world is a foundation for human life to have the fullness of its experience and grow.

Pain, I hope as you read this word again you don't feel SO afraid and some more assuredness that it is okay that pain is part of reality naturally when seen as a response that has to happen and that dealing with it- is simply acknowledging that response fully- That I am alive and I am not a bad thing, I am a human, I am proud of my ability to sense and to feel and experience and have preferences, needs, and wants, that nothing can change that as I am that. That the gratefulness for this entire mechanism of myself can become very real then. So in this lack of denial of what I truly am and always have been you are recognizing the path of true healing.

I have been through the briar patch. I have walked the walk and talked the talk and I hope that this can be used as a catalyst to steer the world in a new direction towards and into the absorption of unconditional Love, some call this the 5th dimension, people like Matt Kahn and Teal Swan*, whom I love so dearly and all the service they have provided for humanity during its healing and growing pains, which are sometimes synonymous. I understand the necessity of pain, once again I will call upon the blessed Mother Mary who appears to me in various ways through blessed women one of them, and perhaps the most memorable to me, Mother Prioress at a local convent or house (a fortress for nuns). She said to me after I told her about my life experiences "God gives us pain to keep us humble."

This is a perspective that may help you heal. It helped me greatly and still does as Truth moves through space and time and can be like a boon or grace wherever we need it. Something my father has said to me is "Hurt people hurt (other) people." How do we reconcile and forgive all this? My own plan for healing is, as you may realize by now, is based on acceptance. I highly recommend Eckhart Tolle and Adyashanti to this end. So, what is acceptance? It is when we can allow the difficulty we are experiencing to be ok. I know that sounds horrific but stick with me. To trust God rather than fear pain.

When you open up to the experience you realize that God within you is bigger and beyond any experience. This is the simplest way of healing. Mooji said "the greatest healing is enlightenment." And that is the simplest way, so continuing on we find that the pain isn't something we have power over. That is the value of acceptance is that we shift into a way of living that is not based in any denial but is a clear seeing but is not to add to our suffering. It is to relieve us from that. So, the main focus that I have adopted is Self-Love (thank you Matt Kahn).

LOG OF MEDIA VIDEO: BY author "Self Love is the way home" (youtube by Joe Vertino)*. I simply put my hand on my heart and repeat over and over "I love you", and it is true it is not false. There is a Gojira song called esoteric surgery in which they sing "You have the power to heal yourself!!"* and another one from Tool is "all this pain is an illusion." Maynard James Keenan is a saint, there is a plain simple awesomeness about him, the lead singer of Tool, the progressive metal band. I saw a video of him in a concert where he did a mass healing.

All he did was allow the experience to be accepted, whatever it is. He had all the crowd together yell or say "Yes!" The last music quote I would like to mention is Tomas Haake of Meshuggah.* He is a lifelong drummer and lyricist. To preface this quote; a lot of our suffering is self-driven unnecessarily, in that case this lyric is relevant. As for the unavoidable pain I will discuss that later on in this passage. "Strive, strive, surmount your obstacles, attain the essence of your goals." The importance of these words is that Tomas Haake is being sarcastic.

He is lashing out at society's standards to constantly unconsciously move without ever thinking for ourselves. Later on in the song he has "To what length would you go to reach your goals? What mantra will you use to justify your means? Who will you betray to secure your dream? What sins will you commit to avoid your sins be seen?" This type of brutal honesty helps me when I am unhappy, in pain. I feel that the lyrics speak for themselves but they also deserve my explanation of them for your benefit.

I understand the power and majesty of music as a source of overflowing compassion and healing potential and divine grace. All of that is possible with the right intent. Once again there is a disdain for society and sarcasm in these words. He is obviously very aware of the pains of living on Earth including the good things, I am sure. So, what is the point? To surrender deeply into the presence of your own light and that is enough. It is simple, it is powerful, it is God. It is healing.

So, why does Love matter? The Dalai Lama said "All people want to be happy and reverse suffering." *

Love is awareness. Love is aware of all experiences. And it is also the complete heart, fully healed. So, this is why Love has the potential to relieve us and to move us in a good way towards perfection and healing, to be fully authentic. I know I am mentioning a lot of my inspirations in this passage but they help me and I hope they can do the same for you. Osho, *the amazing master of yesteryear, is relevant at this point because he is beyond a shadow of a doubt, himself. He is authentic.

He is real. I wish he lived on forever. He was like this purring dragon and had this snarl that could melt any cold heart. He knows how desperately humanity needed a good laugh and to be at peace. He knew his stuff spiritually and also on every other level. He did not ignore pain though. He went through the experience. He, I would go as far to say, would spiritually enjoy it because he knew how valuable it is to removing some illusions. If Pain cannot be detached or prevented from very good or powerful individuals throughout our history then what chance do we have as to disabling it for ourselves? So, in that way we can better understand ourselves, life, and the proper perspective on pain! It is not able to be any other way than what it already is us being life and connected to God and the infinite- but there would be no infinite there without pain being included in Life which we are. It is simply the all in all and God so loves us that we are in that connected to it but don't have power over it or are escaping from it. I pray we can love ourself deeper than any pain, amen. It is ok to fully respond to your own pain- perhaps even outloud like we could call that therapy, bro!

Dr. Frederick P. lenz- a.k.a. Zen Master Rama *

22
THE ABSENCE OF "SELF"

This is an exciting topic to me because I have spent a lot of my own energy moving towards God, and demanding a union as Jesus has. I have watched and listened many times to great souls discussing this and I feel for the people that it just doesn't affect. I am an exception. I feel the immense grace of the sadhguru; when we are open to it we can allow the reality to take over.

When we are living our life from ego, we feel and believe we are separate, separate from everything, this is the nexus of suffering. When we relinquish this limitation on our lives something happens, or everything happens, not just something. There is an undistinguishable essence of Love and being and awareness that doesn't necessarily imply anything. This way of life is not "new" it is prior to "us" as a separate self.

This is the awareness of the creator in us, always in us, through every moment we have been God in an identity that thought it was separate from God itself. The relief and healing vibration of this is imminent and palpable in our experience. We can tune into this through our separate self and eventually we surrender completely to it; the God-ness; aware of nothing but the One reality, which is ultimately satisfying, by the way.

The teacher I would like to mention right now is Zen Master Rama, also known as Dr. Frederick Lenz. He has provided me with a wealth of wisdom but most importantly his voice is ultimately comforting. Some people, students of Zen, believe that the direct path of realization of having no self is found through screams and strikes of a stick on your back or head when doing Za-Zen. But to me (I appreciate the effort) but the gentle approach is much more sincere. I feel that Rama, my trustworthy friend who has lived his last incarnation, has mastered the bliss of comfort. This seems to have come through the perfection of no mind Zen.

He has gone beyond our mind conditioned states and has freed himself to benefit all beings, and I am one of them. He has talked to me through the ethers. The eternal reality is beyond life, death, and conditioned realities.

Speaking from my own experience of no self... I feel that there is an immaculate amalgamation with the present moment. The perfection is one with your experience. That is essentially the basic premise of having no self. And then there usually is a following series of chuckles ranging in intensity, embarrassment, and length.

This is highly recommended to witness on. Mooji has some great ones called "divine laughter" online. VIDEO IN LOG OF MEDIA* So, the main issue a lot people have towards this experience of no self-hood is they feel dangerous because there is a sense of freedom from self, but this does not mean you should have complete disregard. Actually when there is a real lack of ego awareness there is complete peace, not unrest. This is when the being-ness of the Lord settles into your body. We begin to calm down and feel very deeply a longing to love everyone unconditionally.

So, the great allowance of God becomes the present moment for this being. God's Love can be calm in any moment of intensity, that's the power of Love.

So, the ultimate relief of this lifestyle choice is that there is an emptiness, that's it. That's good enough. Then it's as if the pains of life have no ground in your presence of perfect peace and absence of unnecessary concerns.

I challenge the Atheist to take this Zen approach. Move into the abyss, it is your new home. Find out. I trust in reality, do you? …Even in complete nothingness. The musical realm permeates all because when God created she spoke, to speak is a vibration. We exist in and as a vibration of God. We can focus and change our vibration with the love of the cosmic God reality. Music moves us because it is on a deeper level than our identity.

So, the thrill of music can get into our bones, our marrow, and our soul's core. Music can easily transcend our darkness and bring Light. The absence of "small mind" is the dive into the pool of omnipotent graces, where the waters of truth penetrate you deeply and reveal hidden mystery of love and your own majestic qualities. This is the absence of an illusory lifestyle and in exchange for a permanent healing quality. The one. Rather than the many. VIDEO LOG OF MEDIA *"Awareness is not Seperation" youtube video by author in context of this chapter!

The Truth alone. The immortality rather than the crazy senseless perpetuation of misery. Moving forward with courage and powerful grace. This is the absence of self and the empty awareness. What is left when there is no more selfhood? There is all that is dancing in the void space. For me to see God I have only to be God fully. This is the catch, if divinity is alone real then there is nothing else. And then there is enough there to sustain you forever.

Why do we need anymore than God?

Maharaji said "I only need God."* This is what I want for you all. I want you to be at-one with All. The Christ awareness is beautiful in itself, it is beyond the idea of Lack. It is to be completely fulfilled for no reason beyond that it is Real and is aware of its own beauty. This is proof that God loves all that is. And that is enough. A perfect circle. This is why all the saints have a halo because the circle represents completion, in its essence and fullness. To be beyond the realm of choice, an eternal presence that will never be measured or diminished. To be joyful all the time. To be Joy. To become Love. I love you and …you are me. Namaste.

23
RELATIONSHIP(S)

My father has said to me that relationships is what life is about. I do not disagree but I take a completely different approach than his.

My father is an extrovert so he seeks to talk with people almost always, I am an introvert, I do not do that nearly as much. I believe that the experience of relationship is a key ingredient to the stew of joyful living. I personally have experienced relationship in a blank stare manner, meaning that my zen mind is not in need of your thoughts. In this life I have been very attracted to many people, none of which have entered into a relationship with me in a physical manner that was consistent and overall rewarding. I have never been in a "serious" relationship with anyone that you could say is in a physical body.

I am not opposed to this. I feel the need to defend my heart, though, which is not a preferable situation to reside in. I believe that who I am is eternal, so, even though I desire to procreate I am still the all in all walking around and discussing spirituality with you. To have a mind full of awareness is actually a mature way to encounter life and thus relationship, completely. The reason I use this word is because we as individuals are often hiding in illusion. When we open our mind into a more expansive state that fosters the growth and awareness of joy we will experience a more fulfilling relationship paradigm.

If we were going to put relationship into perspective, I often say it is both my laziness and wisdom that creates in me a simple approach. Everything is in relationship in a way. The way you choose to walk on the ground, the way you choose to view your body and your thoughts, and the way that you manage and hopefully enjoy life are all part and parcel of relationship. There is an energy to it. and also how you wish to interact with that energy.

The most obvious understanding of existence is through the energy body (put in references*), or chakras. We are all constantly energy and we move and breathe as that energy, itself. We are using the energy of the universal to create and recreate this experience on Earth today. The key points of relationship are as follows: Trust, vulnerability, self-control, and willingness to change.

These 4 characteristics will enable you to move through any conversation and/or short or long term relationship with more joy.

The love in my heart abides in freedom, when we are working with the energy and deeper calling of the heart we are in right relationship. When we are divorced from our own heartspace we suffer. To be fair, suffering is not wrong, but we must learn to endure and comprehend the spiritual lesson being presented so as to evolve and expand with great energy and love for our life as it is and continues to be.

The relationship I truly desire is with a partner. This is not the case for everyone. Some people will remain celibate, some people will have multiple partners, and some will have one. To some degree we can see that there may not be clear lines between who is a friend and who is a lover, unless we make them ourselves, for ourselves to feel more joy in that clear communication. After all, communication is basically the lynchpin of all relationships, it is required.

So, when you get sick and tired of striving for fulfillment from another form you can be lucky to find the satisfaction of stillness and completeness in this very life. Though you should not look back at the past in disdain you very well may want to.

> The past actions are not deserving of praise nor disdain, the present viewpoint is holy, and the future you create should not cause you worry in the least.

The movement or motivation for one person in and throughout life is wholly their own by definition, it cannot be any other way! So, one good rule to use could be "Are MY relationships in alignment with that fact?" Am I allowing my personal excitement to be the deciding factor? We can take it as far as we can possibly meaning relationship we have with all things, if we use the example of God- we have my own energies and motivation and is this taking priority in this potential discovery of the great I AM in this lifetime? Am I allowing my personality to be completely at ease and exposed as my genuine nature in face of all of the relationship there is in Creation. And knowing that it isn't about quantity so much as it is about quality- and contextualizing the great quest of Life and that no single person we could perhaps ever say is our end of the road but the Lord... and that these beings along it are holy so as to and because of our experience of them and maybe what we experience through them! But, the main spiritual figures I am following seem to be single, so take the conclusion you wish. Thank You.

24
ANGER, FRUSTRATION, AND (UNDERSTANDING) EMOTIONS

So, if I had recorded an entire half on an album and then accidentally deleted it how would that resonate for you? This made me furious at the time. So, how do I deal with this feeling? You tell me, there isn't always a good simple way of making things better, instantly. You just have to return to the surrendered state after you find all the other pathways as unfulfilling or unhelpful. Resting in God you can begin to heal the part of you that feels destroyed. You can take away my life's work but what remains is what is real, nothing else matters ultimately. But good news! What seems to be ultimately real is the unconditional love ~that is God. This is good news for us because that means that ultimately we are love(d).

Anger is very powerful. We have all felt it. I noticed that when anger gives way to surrendered tears and crying we are actually healing rather than hurting. But, there is an essential nature to expressing anger, the way we could do this is with an open heart. For example, remember last time you were very angry and imagine if instead of acting in that moment, which may or may not have been correct, you broke down, cried, became fully open. That to me is a glaring success.

There is so much fear about vulnerability that is really old news and is giving in and transforming into a more honorable way; authentic honesty. Do this: Imagine the world was full of people who had no reason to hide their feelings. Wouldn't that ultimately be a much more joyful place of living, it is where I choose to live and thrive. There will always be more to life, more experiences, more time for understanding, and more people and places, but if we never fully are honest with ourselves and thus with others we are short changing ourselves for no reason at all besides the fear of being weird (see my post, "the importance of being weird").

Frustration is a very unique emotion. It has so much subtlety to it. What I am still working on within my own soul is accepting the unknown aspect of the future without placing too many expectations on myself, others, or the actuality of the circumstances.

So, going back to my original values; the path of acceptance. This is something that deserves its own passage but the idea of this step by step process is a very general and very applicable way of living life, especially during adversity. I hope it helps you. The basic steps are to:

1. See the situation without judgment. Accept it. Don't yet act, only accept.

2. Accept your internal atmosphere <u>about</u> the situation. I know some situations don't allow for this much time in between acting but this helps me.

3. After both the actual physical situation and the emotional landscape have been fully accepted (within reason) then and only then shall you act. This is not always possible but it isn't a bad practice to use for the simple reason of more joy and less pain.

Emotions are divine. Just sit with that. Emotions... are... divine. We are so concerned with how to change them we don't see the blessing in them. This is a huge step forward for many people to shift the mindset from lack to abundance. The attempt to get rid of our lack emotions gives way to the acceptance they are in abundance. From concern to excitement. From control to surrender. From ignorance to enlightenment. From darkness to Light. And seeing LOVE all along the way as a parent or spouse holding your hand or perhaps even a child (God takes many forms). Really, it takes all forms.

Well, then now that we can move into this perspective (just a strong suggestion for inner peace to abound). Would you prefer no emotions in your life over the sometimes reckless feelings? Would you prefer to be absent of attachment BUT still connected to the joy of experiencing life completely? This is what I am interested in. Emotions are ways of perceiving that are an intrinsic aspect of being alive. So, instead of trying to banish them like a demon we can embrace them like a child. We can accept them first, then they pass away smoothly. We learn from them. We grow through them. We ultimately can use them as a backdrop for a solid meditation to see more clearly the reality of God.

Anger is not quite an emotion but it can be confusing perhaps we can say clearly because of parents ignorance and unfortunately "solid" mentality... when they are adamant when you cannot be adamant ... you are a little child guaranteed you weren't! WE WERE! So if you want a logical reason we know for a fact anger is not an emotion is because if you became angry right now in defense of this just-mentioned ignorance- that would be attempting to destroy the entire analysis in greatness and vulnerability of ALL THE EMOTIONAL BODY. Therefore anger is not an emotion it has no service in it- It is also just like worry... But we can see that frustration is natural response to circumstances in total and can at least be said as is rational and can be understood perhaps in its rootedness and further on its will, its agenda, and its meaning.

Anger is an intentional act of the opposite of kindness it is directed outwards. Worry is an intentional act of the opposite of kindness directed toward ourself/inward. We can be certain both are intentional after we have read this and you have read so you technically are excuseless!

Gratefulness also is not an emotion but it is an intentional and sometimes spontaneously arising completely appropriate experience that can complete the human being - which allows the emotional body to be respected as best as we can.

> This proper perspective on life * leads to the divine path of Christ which we can say we know for certain (again that word) has forgiveness in it and all throughout it.

You simply begin to heal well and live and make better decisions on all levels when you respond appropriately as your entire emotional body is and always does.

Emotions our emotional body cannot be wrong just like us having simply a body cannot be wrong either, friend, dear whom I love. The way to truly move forward in the most appropriate way is on the level of the soul that you are (eternally). The true joy comes from moving not in aversion and the most relevant possible way to understand that is only emotions... even they say "motion" in their divine and meant-to-be name!

JUST LIKE WE ARE MEANT TO BE! WE may not know the emotions Jesus Christ experienced except through our own divine intimacy with our own heart and our own soul and our field of feelings that are inevitably and intrinsically intertwined within it thus- those that we all are. And further we know from Christ's very speech - it is made known unto us we are meant to be just as he is and was in the most respectful way of authenticity throughout all time and space. So, we feel something we even have confusing perhaps abusive relationships in which during and hopefully after we bring into the space of Christ in our shared world called a Church and present our bare emotions literally only to Christ who remains in that solid frame as the Divine reality beyond our understanding forever yet we TRUST him.

I hope this instills the proper perspective in you for the rest of time about that which you may even want to identify with - EMOTIONS. But as we know from Lord Buddha there is a need for the great relief of relinquishing our own fateful flame for the sake of the eternal one that is only cosmic and cannot go like this feeling it is an emotion it is our body it is me dying it is me having an orgasm it me thinking I'm God it is me... it is me alone in a room... and that's it!

This great relief is final Nirvana. The thing about emotions is we can never control them but we have free will yet- psychology has this basically figured out for it is simple that we have an eternally innocent self which is inner child and we have an adult self which temporarily protects and provides for itself which includes the inner child in this very lifetime. This is how we can work with ourself, our own Dharma which we have read about earlier in this book and GOD so much in this great manifesto completely and utterly and proudly forever no matter what about centered around that I AM- that is why we have computers and libraries with memories and children etc. The difference between sin and emotions is the proof unto ourselves as humans on and on why emotions are always natural and beneficial and we can assert are divine and our choices are not always- but yet emotions are involuntary... Meditation does not get rid of emotions... Prayer does not give us more emotions... But **understanding** is the most necessary grace for us all strictly only about them; EMOTIONS.

There is a very clear truth exposed here the same one in two places; that is an indication of what it means/comes from being human, the segment "6: The Shadow" also has it there in. The point of it (all) is UNDERSTANDING in both places, which is the same in that it is ourself a human, emotions and the shadow both want just recognition and the overall goal is communication- that it is literally for us to live at all without communication. One proof is that every human has emotions and that emotion is our internal communication and we listen to our own and then we can try to express our own and more toward outward to others and then listen to theirs- it is such a silly thing to go against that.

25
ORGANIZED RELIGION AND GOD

I recently picked up a new book "God without religion". * I am only a chapter or so into it but the basic premise is obvious and well received. The importance and relevance of this timely subject is thus: I have a friend in India who believes that Hinduism is the one true religion, I also have a friend in my hometown who feels the same way about Christianity. This is a secret big issue that will take real love to solve, together. To me the answer lies in this anecdote; I was once one morning listening to a talk of the Dalai Lama, the ocean guru (Tenzin Gyatso). *

In this talk he was discussing many subjects and responding to questions, at one point during this phrase to phrase translation he said the words "the ultimate reality" and as soon and while those words were spoken I felt it, I knew it as Truth.

This ultimate reality may have come through a Buddhist leaders mouth and heart but had nothing to do with any religion, specifically. This is my answer, the only issue I have at this moment is how do I communicate this to you in so many words. Though this is a background issue compared to a lot of the things we put our mind upon to me this is a serious one. We know what we are capable of and we know that the belief system has a lot of influence.

Something I always say is God cares more about showing us love than God cares about us being "right". But we seem to sometimes have this flip flopped, few think we will be fully loved once we have done what is "right". This is the heart of the issue of all organized religions. Jesus mentioned in the Gnostic Gospels, which were edited out of the "official" Bible for no good reason, that "My [real] church is not made of sticks and stones" (The gospel of Thomas).*

Jesus Christ, the one who is supposedly and meant to be the basic inspiration for the entire religion of Christianity, said this. This means the church is not a building, it is not closer to us when we are being baptized or when we are listening to the priests speaking surrounded by big marble arches. The Lord's heart is the church Jesus was talking about, he and the Lord are One, this is the Truth and motivating factor for Jesus' entire lifetime and is basically what he referred to as salvation.

So, how do we heal our minds from a blanket of past ignorance in respect to organized religion besides being completely over it? We can choose to come into God's presence, we can ask God about it or we can try it out if God's Love is dependent on anything or if it isn't at all.

We can test out the Truth, this is really our birthright and this is why organized religion and certain people claiming to have some grasp on the "truth" as opposed to us all being equal in the Truth is actually extremely detrimental to our overall joy and growth. Good news! You are reading this and absorbing the good vibes, hopefully. I am writing this, good for me.

And I would hope that you would feel like the Truth in this book can be part of your life and times. Trust your heart.

The great souls that have helped me recently and will continue to are Maharaji,* Indian saint and guru of Ram das(s) and Krishna das (by the way, why does Krishna das's name have one "S" but Ram Dass's has 2?, haha). And also Babaji, the premavatar and lineage master of Paramhansa Yoganandaji, whom I believe is the yogi teacher of ALL Americans. These beings and lineages understood the great Truth and perfect Love and glory of God throughout the ages of ancient times and I am overjoyed and honored to share their immense presence and wisdom with you now.

VIDEO IN LOG OF MEDIA * There is a video on Babaji that can be found and enjoyed on In this video it became very instantly obvious to me why I was so soulfully attracted to Babaji, specifically at this time, is because he preached and believed in the transcendence and eventual dissolution of all barriers between us and the divine radiance of the creator. Babaji to me is a very pure being and may have been the teacher of Jesus! How lovely and humbling for all the Christians. Big hugs.

Maharaji,* also known as Baba Neem Karoli essentially understood the deep love of Christ and of the different religious figures throughout ancient times. This is a man that has the nicest grip on my soul. I have been going through a lot lately and he has single-heartedly provided me with a constant subtle yet powerful support that is obvious and appreciated by me and I pray it continues.

So, Maharaji's raw power of love is the real miracle, though I was born in America and the culture here is Christian, predominantly, God felt it was necessary for me to understand him differently. He brought me to the guru's feet and showed me the reality of divine Love that is beyond time, space and form and ultimately any one religion. I love you and may God continue to guide you on your honorable journey. Om shanti Ram. The reason Babaji was mentioned to give one is that our shared world needs order, organization, religion, and God and to give a simple and foundational living gaze to it all. We know that the organized religion is entirely constructed by humanity and that God is not. We know that just as ethics exists in our shared universe we know that the justice system is designed to act out that exact thing and yet it is man made also, the same comparison; it is a just word it is a righteous word to use "comparison" like with heaven.

This dilemma really the only dilemma we have in this title is the lack of relaxation and the lack of awareness on a solely individual plane. Not to judge you all no matter if you like to be called humans or not. But my attempt is to bring light into our hidden darknesses as mentioned in the introduction. The simplicity of God is forever and it should be magnified through organized religion. The good step for every individual is to step back (if needed) and see for yourself organized religion from as if you are at home and comfortable and have nothing to impress or repress. And allow the natural experience to occur and continue that way for all of time. This authentic fellowship you have begun with this human construct is long-lasting and heavenly it is just and wholly your own- which is such a pleasant and prioritized and important tenant or principle of ALL organized religion.

This dharma we have always of connecting with the divine takes its time throughout our lifetimes. And if we understand this great point is that organized religion appears in certain ways throughout as the divine whether we are Jewish or Sudanese or Albanian. This dharma to connect with God as God is always available and perfect the organized religion allows our lives to be aligned and organized to that great way that great dharma forever- and if we begin and continue to develop this proper perspective really just on life plainly we become established in our authentic self and also would rid all the possible churches of any illnesses of the mind that may be presenting themselves or not presenting themselves.

"There seems to be a clear twist in my beard about organized religion still as I felt and I am naturally all about the Truth we can say" says some people, though I may have not found it yet. Or I may have found some of it, I may have found it in a nasty way, I may have found it in only myself and not in others or I may have found it from having a horrible experience facilitated by organized religion. I may have been convinced I was wrong about it being found by everyone else, whether in church or not in church. I may be struggling and be so confused because of the atmosphere of a big church that seems to strangely belittle the ACTUAL HUMAN. The wondrous rapture of God while ignoring the sermon happened from my own effort alone to crane my neck and stare at the stained glass windows with a royal purple and ended up being the only thing raising my spirit above where it was earlier albeit in the beautiful sunshine upon the entrance.

I am honored to resonate with Truth and the Truth is I prefer gentleness and I prefer perfume and I prefer stillness and reflection and I prefer my own personal agenda in perpetuity above the crowd's. I prefer to express rather than not. I prefer to learn rather than attempt to do anything otherwise forever! I have resolve on my own. I am a man, a woman, a child, I am seemingly away from God from time to time and simply love the idea of their being a place that represents his holy omnipotence in which I am utterly involved. I recognize God and therefore I am technically already and forever bound to a Church in this very lifetime!

I am able to heal myself with Reiki - I am able to act on my own highest excitement and perhaps laugh through the failures all life long without any chastisement by any firmly established body and its members like a Priest! I do have a compass inside- and I do willfully never deny it perhaps- I am not a slave to this thing called organized religion even though it can be seen as good and bigger than myself. I am not in need therefore of its DESTRUCTION. I am enabled and enabling says all the caretakers and chair putter users and step sweepers and statue maintainers … I am in the church and know enough of myself and of the world and its needs to carry on doing my holy dharma which is to give way to free will and are sure the church is ready for those who will come to it.

God this whole time reading watching us… and to appease our humans creates and send angels of great beauty and proportion that bring our attention home to ourself- as the ascetic the Yogi and the mystic the hermit those who don't participate en masse understand as their dharma in this very lifetime. I love you and I am so proud to be a Reiki master healer- Usui and to have written and been enabled by GOD to inspire and assist you with them and this work; manifesto.

26
WORK AND DISCIPLINE

The third Reiki Principle : "Just for today ... I will do my work honestly"

We know that work is not going anywhere and that work is not a person with opinions or beliefs and that is ALWAYS our calling for it to be done with honesty as our centering force. Like Gods work is to have gravity and the rest occurs through its manifestations, of what we can now call planets aligning and misaligning and sharing in their chosen spaces and bigger places and for some time it been about and forevermore with some clout does not seem too far off.

The obvious fact to me is that work just like our attitude and personal preferences are not burdensome but they are instilled in us, as we are created from time and time again as humans and we may resonate with such

Work and Discipline

wondrous things as starseeds* as mentioned in the earlier chapters of this book. But we can recognize for ourself that discipline is such a uniquely individual experience- that when stuck inside the sacred human heart chakra becomes a two sided flame that purifies both the inside world and the outside world.

It has no other agenda to its name for good for all. The root being discipline as we now can see it clearly we have a less mean or hurtful way of thinking about work, more self-loving and accurate for we are its creator and maintainer. We are its systemic manufacturer in fact. Everyday we wake up we are re-creating the already manifested world as it is in our shared world. The genuine approach to (all) life is what we desire inherently and that is like mud on the Earth and the undeniable must be present while we are at work - thus the most important word being honesty with work!

There is no way to escape or exchange it like a street in a car... The driver is you and the future is unknown and the past well it may be horrid but we can say it useful to our present for sure! WE are first and foremost decision makers nothing before it lies anywhere throughout all of creation! Us humans, we decide! The only thing worthy of our decision is to bring about our own personal change - like a new simple day. This is the agenda of the universe and since we are in need of help that is why you are reading this here and now with Dr. Joe Vertino (author), an expert on the field of healing- for you deserve no less, amen. Going forward does mean you can think like a snake an animal you may have never been allowed to resonate with in your own mind up to now- that the swerving may have felt abusive and offensive through life but when you realize you can take control of the whole ship you are designating alone you are letting go of (all) denial and the Swerves become less burdensome and more appropriate in their scope and understanding.

That these societal blockades can be explored or simply avoided or eventually changed. But that can't ever really be ignored. And when we designate our attention to simply achieving the goals we are able to get through one swerve around something when we wish there was nothing there at all. But never the less we should be proud of ourself to demonstrate unto ourselves what it is we truly are throughout our day. And the fulfillment we are seeking externally and/or circumstantially can be made real internally alone. And that is Life- we can seek and know - but it must be seen and done as humans. So what it is is the activation of our truest self.

The fear of the world not being perfect or secure right now needs to end definitely! In you there reader, I can say at least take heart in me. Ah. For I am here with you and given you guaranteed sound wisdom and practical life advice for all the ages there will be. The problem being is when Humanity fears their own decision making nature.

The way of the world is really only so far as the way of each individual which is to be brought unto the light of our awakenings and what fosters them. The bliss of the saints is found there in; it takes the Trust of your sincerity to accomplish this! And you can begin that journey now. And know that God knows everything! The beauty that you are should not be feeling like it has to be proven at work- What this means is that that little girl or boy who is you now is certainly capable of so much more than when they were little and now. And they are even able to teach other children. The true friend of you remember is honest work and that there is no wrong in being so determined to find what that is, BUT A MOST important prayer is simply the grace of paying attention to yourself and sensitive to what only is your business to make sure you find out what that is as soon as you can. And the reasons for life become clearly only your own. I love you, just like in the earlier chapters, haha.

The importance of work is for some obvious reasons; we have to do it. We have things that have to be done to maintain life on this plane of existence. With that being said and accepted to the best of our ability we can begin to move forward. My father once said "I work to live not live to work." * The idea of this is that we are not slaves rather we are sovereign beings in this cosmic soup and on some other "higher" level we chose to come here, and spread some of our juicy soul goodness on the Earth, Gaia as she has been known.

Discipline is an important step in existence just as work is. Discipline is necessary for us to mature and to have some civility but where discipline gets good is when it becomes an innate quality in us and for us. For example, joy and prayer and a constant obedience to God's will are best when they come spontaneously and naturally going along with the present moment rather than against it, which is sometimes unavoidable. So, when meditating you can see and feel the movements of energies within and even around you when you sit or after a while. You then can decide to discipline yourself and to remain still regardless of them or you can interact with them, either way is good for you. Discipline in this sense is necessary if you have some goal in mind, for example, enlightenment.

So, if you don't care about that then just enjoy your silent sitting. But for those "disciples" who move with discipline; the goal is just as real as your desire to attain it.

So, inevitable as it is that I come to some spiritual conclusions I will try to make some very practical and applicable statements about work in general devoid from spiritual experiences. I have experienced manual labor and some work situations that were quite unpleasant as well as some more new experiences that are quite lovely. I believe that if we separate work in our minds from other experiences we might be doing something strange in our mind. So, in my experience we have some reason for doing what we are doing to some extent. So, the next thing I would like to say about work is that I truly believe and actually I know that it is meant to be joyful, just as joyful as our days off of "work".

To me work is a very general idea that we seem to be quite obsessed with here. I feel that if it causes more pain than pleasure than we should consider dropping it all together. But, of course, people will still be active in doing the things and activities that inspire them to live. They will chop the wood and carry the water, as they say in Zen. They will maintain but since when is maintaining supposed to be painful? Never is the answer to that.

So, I know of communities that have a self-sustaining circle of life, from the dirt and the seeds to the laundry and the chanting and the yoga and the nature time. This is possible and actually may be much more in alignment with the divine than a 9 to 5 job in some metropolis, God bless you people anyways.

Nowhere in the definitions of work and/or of discipline does it say experience a lot of pain. So, why do we seem to suffer? I believe that the sense of gratitude and surrender to something that we happen to be going through is my most consistent answer if that even is an "answer". But I feel that we may be mature enough to accept our relationship with the world and its state but also be wise and aware and kind enough to desire to create change for the future, in which the idea of work can not be so ominous and can be more light and pleasant but just as necessary.

A Buddhist monk in bright ocher.

27
DEATH

The hot topic for many spiritual teachers seems to be death. It is as inevitable as the spring rain and also as unpredictable. It has a hold on our minds and mortality but then why are we so fascinated with it if it is something that we aren't beyond? In reality death is constant just as life is constant: The ultimate paradox, or perhaps the most obvious one. The movement from one moment into a new one is both death and life. I will explain this further; the past dies and in those ashes the birth of the future explodes into creation. So, that to me is enough explanation of death but I am sure we want to know about the big sleep, physical death process and completion. This is something that can only be experienced by pure consciousness.

Ram Dass* also known as Dr. Richard Alpert recently physically passed away. He had an experience when he was younger that was similar. He had taken a drug and was experiencing the drug and as he was sitting on a couch… He saw form disappear. But he still was experiencing this, so that means that the physical body is not the ultimate experiencer. So this is why if you were to talk to angels or aliens about death they would make it seem very ordinary because they understand that it is not as real as consciousness, in the end. We all are One; this is the reality of God, our souls come from God and return to God's heart. This is beyond duality as the master Babaji teaches. *

So, is this good for us or bad for us or does it not matter one iota or is it "the point?" I don't know but I would like to say that I love you no matter what you say or feel. I believe that the universe can be experienced as a mirror and also can be a very visceral experience, both. But I feel that within all the suffering there is something called grace that does not care what we believe or really anything about us, it just happens, love happens, it is not always because we pray or because we go to church or got enlightened somehow.

So, to me death is the illusion of change but once we see what doesn't ever change then we don't really worry so much about ourselves but we only want to bring people to that realization, somehow someway someday some night. So, this is the great debate to me: Why did the Siddhartha Guatama,* the Buddha who woke up under the Bodhi tree choose, completely on his own, to attempt to spread enlightenment? He realized the absolute beyond form and time and death and I dare say beyond life… he was seriously considering not doing a thing for the rest of eternity but something moved him, this would have been a passive suicide. ~And he decided with full free will and awareness to get up and walk to a town to tell people about the reality of God realization, and so the universe moved with him. Love motivated him.~

One more chunk of words on death… silence is our closest experience to death. When we are ready for reality to come to us it will, most likely in silence and acceptance of our own divine nature. In a silence that doesn't even mind if your mind is a blaze with random thoughts. This penetrating silence is exactly like having sex with God without the aftermath to clean up. I love you, dear one, we all want pleasure but it comes in different ways.

So, another explanation of a paradox coming up is that silence is empty; how can it have form so as to penetrate us? This isn't possible? Is it? Well, reality doesn't have to play by our rules, our fake rules, it is as it is. The wisdom I have is to respect reality, and to see something for its own sake. This means to open your eyes and stare. And most likely you will feel a smile spreading across your beautiful visage. Maybe the most real smile you ever showed to the world, and then if you're lucky maybe a few tears, maybe you will surrender some ego, maybe you will disappear and experience life from the perspective of loving awareness. Who knows?

> Well as a sacred spacious Buddhist Teacher who is available unto all souls- without mentioning more or less - let us get a clarifying perspective on Death! The realization of death (not meaning its manifestation and eternal consequence) is best to come unto the developing human at a natural swing a cosmic swing like of a golf club, perhaps a highschooler at golf club- as opposed to really another "way" and there really is no other way because no one is really intending to injure the soul- but it is never really appropriate for us to play "the universe itself" or "God." BUT we must realize we die- and that is all this point is.

The "hope for enlightenment" a very BUDDHIST CHANT/SONG has been presented to me from above and within the world we are in - here it is; the link: a wonderfully made video *LOG OF MEDIA

"If we wish to properly and positively conceptualize Death";

An aside by Dr. Joe Vertino that is serious: (even if you don't understand poetry or so you think right now please do read it like in school for its meddle alone! To be born; read it like how if you "don't like" babies- the way you look at babies- read it).

My Own Religion: The Power of Love

..take heart but nothing with you take heart but nothing with you- that's all; dear souls... "Over there " - it yells out

And a silence not a stillness ... within me arose- for it wasn't done through my efforts!

Then I stare but not glare for there is no object to see, I wish I dream. On.

I love to see.. OVER .. THERE... THERE IS ANOTHER SHORE ! A BIG SMILE A BIG SMILE ARISIES WTHIN ME IT SURELY WASNT JUST FOR ME!

The man who has been trying to listen is... " listen the over shore the other shore ... shove offfff, love" it says again- like a slavery song of freedom- that stuff ain't going anywhere that southern history- it really happened they were made slaves and they were real life from "elsewhere" !

The deer in the field I wanted to file them away, I ran "into your arms" but I really just ran into a tree with my car not my arms, I wished SO HARD ... but in reality there was nothing inside of my wishing well, and now I am just a puddle of mudd... I loved ...

I am like shifting sand now, I am relaxing, and soon I will be no more, BUT BEFORE YOU, I shall perish... I shall fail for I was afraid failure ah I am getting nowhere with you this lifetime, hahaha.. I smoked so much too.... Father you don't watch me you don't watch me. I am eager to learn next .... One!

"The other shore is no more for I am compassion and I have no tail!" Something shows up like a Sprite- it spake.

"The other shore was the way to go- it was something to do called dharma and it brings the soul erect with passionate blood that it does not let drip away and away..and awayyyyy soooo* ...

Then as you go nowhere it becomes Light. You have suddenly appeared on the other side - I am very real - you. All done die alone forever!"

(end of aside) ..

(Now) the aside is done * But you may be erect with bloody passions- may the rest of your time ON EARTH be dharmic! Angels are like yay.

The death, about it is nothing. Know that there is nothing that is ever ABOUT it. Ah, so now you are alive and you are obliged to not endure but to possess your experience. The responses ; ... all of them are your job to embrace that come up - I can say, in response to "DEATH"!

The joy of creation is to free. My known dharma is freeing just as it is being known by others, further, to assert because it is true and real like all of our lives are.

The death is not the problem nor is it able to be overcome- but it is available to us that there is a substance to existence - and its recognition is palpable and needed not only for "survival" but for thriv-al or thriving and for the ultimate journey and destination of TRUE JOY!

With this knowledge in our hearts may we sharpen our swords. With this grinning winning authorship may I be slain appropriately in this life- and may I remain dead and may my words remain written. That's all. That's all, bless all. BUT LORD< so many have come before me a trampling forward and presented themselves with all greatness available to them with blessings inside and have found me still Lord right here - to give way to the purpose divine of these words that manifest from ear to ear first and then hit like fingers on the book.. May it be read! Amen - was it humanity or you who decided it wasn't good enough the them ... in the such glorious *away* as the past. I defer to you that's why I ask and write it so!

The splendid giving way to resilience and more splendid and then nothing by the bay and sheer manifestation in which I have relation or correlation... and unto death I am somehow relevant and ready .... Still ... I am stilll.... Like a calm water.

Do you remember those current people in the past who dreamed of remaining dead forever. And yet was there impulse pure was it somehow a stealing away from you?

I am adorable says the human mind Lord, I have manifested and have seen, right away. I seem to know what is so potent like a fire and I can find others like myself ... about. I am learning humility now and succumbing to nature slowly in total and by myself, too, and I know I die.

As a Buddhist teacher I must say- my only work of poetry as a whole book is strictly (also) my only work that is declaratively (labeled) Buddhist.

I have succeeded at my quest to simultaneously have and possess real and worthy experience and not befriend death... but rather or ALSO glaringly received grace of which there is a Lord and the allowance of it- infinity, I shook hands!

"Becoming friends with Infinity" * LOG OF MEDIA

by Joseph Vertino (youtube)

please watch and SHARE

I am a professional Spiritual Guide, author, and musician, and Reiki Master Healer - Usui! I love the Truth which drove me to make this video for us all ! - May the personal will be subdued enough to be (again) curious and made sweet by exploring what is technically always on our personal tongue - Infinity!

A Bible quote:

> **Revelation 6:1-8**
> Now I saw when the Lamb opened one of the seals; and I heard one of the four living creatures saying with a voice like thunder, "Come and see." And I looked, and behold, a white horse. He who sat on it had a bow; and a crown was given to him, and he went out conquering and to conquer.

This quote is brilliant in the sense of it has what brings attention to itself like a shining Lamp or contemporary flashlight. It reminds of the Emerald Tablets of Thoth; Hermes Tresmisgistus.

"The ability to transcend death is nill but the ability of the human and the calling forth of it; to be in awe of God; is not and its UNDOING is nill!"

Archangel Azrael bless us all- The archangel of Death and Mental Stability.

28
PETS, ANIMALS, AND CREATURES OF ALL KINDS

We all have seen some cats, dogs, lizards, and probably fish and gerbils. But what purpose do you feel they serve for humanity or how can we better serve them and God at the same time?

One great explanation I have heard of Dogs and cats thanks to * Matt Kahn is that both species are for our household and familial benefit. Cats are supposed to clean our energy, removing from us useless energies and transmuting them allowing us to feel less stress and more calm. Dogs, working on the same team but in a different way, are simply there to generate joy within us and obviously a sense of physical protection for us as guardians of our households. This is a very simple perspective and I know that all creatures do more than just serve one purpose for us and for the universe. Dogs and cats also help us to come into our communal present moment, which is very valuable and reason enough for us to choose to live with them. I would like to add to this: Dogs represent the masculine energies and cats represent or project the feminine ones, this helps for a more balanced home, and, potentially a more balanced existence at large.

Two of the most beautiful people, *Cesar Milan, the dog whisperer and Eckhart Tolle, the spiritual teacher and avid dog lover, met together perhaps for the first time in an interview which is available through the wonders and divine purpose of the internet. This interview is heartfelt and highly recommended whether you want to enlighten yourself or cherish animals more or both.

Here it is- Link for interview video (youtube.com): LOG OF MEDIA

Eckhart Tolle understands the primary ground and field of pure being and how humans are in one sense above the animals because of our apparent dissociation from this way of living when we are obsessed with our thoughts which dogs and some other animals are not yet capable of. We can find some solace and relief in the company of animals like cats and dogs to return to this state of pure being, absent of overthinking.

We seem to be on a consciousness bridge between indigenous or more animal-like realm and the Christos consciousness of enlightened being that has consciously moved beyond ego thought and once again returned to pure being. As for *Cesar Milan I have watched all of his episodes on Netflix and I absolutely adore him and his special and important work.

The more esoteric side of animals and even some more mystical creatures are also a large part of my interest for this specific post and actually occupy a lot of my mind on a daily basis. I believe that coming into proper alignment with one's animal nature can actually be very beneficial for our overall health and spiritual healing. God may be formless but God also can appear to us a beautiful Lioness or a running white wolf and that should be revered as such. One spiritual practice I may recommend to you is to see all as God, for example to see everyone around you as *Jesus, Mother Mary, or St. Joseph, this takes some practice and is actually a meditation exercise but can greatly and rapidly increase the size of the heart and generate much compassion and healing energies all with God's grace and peace.

The necessity of care is dearly related to our relationship with all earth's creatures for we have to accept the responsibility of our state as the most active and influential species on this earth; humanity. So, we actually are just as dependent if not more dependent on the other creatures as they are with us- would we be not sadder without them than thus them without us- animals, think about it. We may have a higher intelligence quotient but what does that matter if we are single handedly ruining some of the earth? A perspective I would like to share is the balance between the spiritual evolution and the technological or material evolution.

Any race that exists in the cosmos must develop a balance between the spiritual or ethical side and the technological or raw scientific side and it seems to me to be obvious that if the spiritual or ethical side is below the other than that species will inevitably fail. It is just a theory but it may be better if it were true, who knows? So, the reason for this is with great power comes great responsibility, as exemplified by Peter Parker of Spiderman.

If we felt like expanding our consciousness here we could talk cosmic evolution with other forms of life that have most likely gone beyond our own intelligence but the ones we are interested in here are those that have come to understand the oneness principle of the cosmos. So, any Extra-terrestrial that comes to you through God is welcome. I believe that * Drunvalo Melchizedek is right when he stated that the vast majority of the evolved life in our cosmic soup are benevolent.

What a relief. But we have some work to do both inner and outer to move beyond this place in our existence and evolution to become aware of how we fit in to God's infinite creation but rather than the motivation being to avoid annihilation rather I think we could be motivated by our own innate desire to grow and to enjoy more and fully. To perpetuate love and indulge somewhat in our own curious nature.

A few words on 'curiosity'; when I was young, a boy in my backyard, I was absolutely fascinated by all creatures and especially insects, for the most obvious reason of my size and theirs, it was like the universe put them there for me to learn from. I would simply adore them and I was not afraid of them even though I knew they may sting. I remember studying their moves, their path through the grass. I believe the curiosity factor is very important for joy, for humans and maybe universally also. I resonate with the energy of joy and so I bring all things into that and conversely remove the obstacles.

The humbling insight: God lives just as much within every animal as within us no matter how special we seem to be or how far we can shoot ourselves into space. The greatest gift seems to be selfless service, for example when and if we explore space safely one day we are destined to assist other species (the way we have been assisted). I feel it is more valuable to teach to other less evolved species than it would be for us to selfishly ignore them and keep them in suspense about the true grandeur and wonder of our shared home; the stars. By this I mean we would educate and be educated in this cosmic soup. And us remembering our times on this Earth now in this very insightful and exciting age we can access our past and find deep compassion and empathic love for those truly foreign civilizations whose home may be other galaxies in our single universe!

The truth about creatures is that we are all creatures. I believe sometimes the lines between imagination and reality can be confusing. When we may be exploring the multi-dimensional realities we can encounter creatures and this is part of the fun. For example, mermaids, yetis, and dragons may all be real. But to find this as an extension of ourselves we can see with wisdom rather than judgment and enjoy the cosmos with a child-like curiosity.

On a soul level we can see that incarnations as a dragon may not be so far-fetched. I remember my relative once told me she had a dream of a night before she got pregnant that a white dragon appeared to her and asked if he, the dragon, could be her child, she said yes. This is the way I see creatures, they represent the potential beauty of our own existence. My twin flame once said to me "the beauty you see in me is a reflection of yourself." So next time you watch dolphins swim out into the sunset remember that. God may be formless but the divine will use form to show the immaculate beauty of its existence to those who care to see it and perhaps even write about it, or... to become it.

> The point of beauty that must be presented is that beauty is actually important! I say it that way because we do not know that going into our serious experiences we can fall apart like a little flower- except the flower is supposed to fall apart... and it is just our job to learn about ourself and/also in combination with everything (else)! So, this is why and where beauty is so crucial/important is because when we include ourself into our education base we are naturally encouraging what we recognize (collectively?) As pure and righteous which is Spirit!

Then as we encourage study of ourself and of the other(s) too we are putting things into proper alignment like the stars in the cosmic deep. And we are becoming more complete by not pushing away something like our individual (self) for the sake of some low self-image bullshit that produces great imbalance and potential disaster by focusing likely scientifically outward - and disregarding the people, the subjective realm of (all the) people - and then also it gets really probably hellish because we are caught in a loop of attempt of Self-actualization through means of external achievement on which also we could assert that survival is dependent because it is empirical science yet we are also caught in the loop of our emotional and/or self -image development being invested in the "success" of the external scientific objective realm or work!

So, you can see how our efforts to be educated are non-resistant of the other ones. That the proper use of our current lifetime is self-determined and a natural logical conclusion in sight of that single important fact is to study that in which you are involved in and bound to with great reverence and respect! Your personal highest excitement!

So, animals certainly do not take away from this pursuit of Gods after our souls and developing (constantly) in our Spirit's. I perceive REVERENCE as the single most important thing possible- even though we cannot know everything ahead of time! The reason is found in that there is SUCH purpose and SUCH awareness in all of us and we all only individuals move through life we as beings who honor thee animals around us are producing in our single selves the cosmic intention of growth which translates in language as reverence!

So, even though we may not know much about what important or public certain ones of our kind say (is)- we in our personal lonely and private life are still involved universally, which we must be as by way of being born in our habitable Earth bubble. This can show us the resonance of which we can bring our whole, holy, and wholesome attention into it... like a single point on which the particles of our mind can seem like magnetic of one pole made into dust and attracted to the other pole which is (still) a solid 3d object.

That being right living; in the eightfold path in Buddhism there is one known as RIGHT MIND- right mind is to be established in a correct posture in your own psyche - of which you live your life and become more adept at it acquiring positive karma with or without touching other people's lives! The sensitivity we have toward all life can manifest by simply taking serious the lives of our pets, animals, and creatures. So how we choose to relate to these creatures we are able to put it into context that we are not meant to be around all of them or them to be wrongfully manipulated to suit us, individual humans, and yet they exist and we exist so this true knowledge in context of our life with our pets enables us in our soul to naturally become more karmically aligned and the universal way of all the worlds begins to manifest and can find a home on our personal heart chakra and experience of life! Then we can fulfillingly resonate with the Universal love when taking care of our personal pets, and when experiencing with animals and creatures of all kinds- thanks to and for thee lovely Earth!

In all our ordinary ways we can plumb the depths of the shared Universe and perhaps in that way alone we are removing any blockages inside our own self-life between me and proper attainment of goals; success! Nirvana is the "Ultimate Real" that the soul craves onward as it goes! So, we should put into context that the successes in our apparently ordinary lives are to be seen and made near and dear to our soul's heart (chakra) - at least- it is OUR JOB OBVIOUSLY TO MAKE THAT THE CASE!

The joy is always meant to be fully experienced and I feel so sad for the souls who were denied that - the Absolute is still very much Immaculate and our recognition of that, like when we go into a church, is also thee "Ultimate Real" and we can make our own way, our own Religion, in which we are not destroying or attempting to destroy our shared world or others (experiences) but rather prioritizing the agenda of our soul and its growth- of which the only real requirement is "Self- Trust", which can very quickly become, self- respect, self-awareness, and self- protection especially if we are in need of escaping certain circumstances and then "I" not "we" give in to the Power of Love!

This we can say translates, to God too, as saving yourself! What a close and intimate experience over and over again that you need to perfect - ask any genuinely happy soul- ask any person who when in the grips of their great acts what was their internal experience?

If the Creator had a thought about this topic; it would look like this!-with arms wide open.

29
DIVINE RELATIONSHIPS

In actuality every relationship is divine because it is all going to the same place - God. The relationships we so furiously experience are used and designed by the universe to create more expansion. So what is expansion and what does it matter to us in the here and now? The universe is always expanding, and as the universe is in direct relationship with us on a constant basis so we too are expanding and if we are stuck the universe knows some tricks to help us out, like metamucil or roto-rooter.

You could say that this book is one of them. That is one reason, the other reason is that growth and prosperity are the way of the worlds, using passion and excitement to create new realities to open new pathways, music, art, and poetry have the innate power to do this almost instantaneously, I pray that the ease with which musicians can manifest energetic change can be also adopted by other fields of work because, in reality, we are in relationship always. When we are walking down the street we are in relationship with our thoughts or when we are staring at the sky we are in relationship with the emptiness. When newness comes into our field of awareness we are in a relationship with the unknown. Isn't that lovely to know about our potential partners in and throughout our lifetime?! "Claro que si!" In Spanish means- of course, yes!

This may not be the perspective you were thinking of when you read the topic but it is true and just different - give me a chance to convince you. Also I must admit I have, up to this point, never been in a serious romantic relationship with anybody in a body alive this time on earth. But I write on divine relationships nonetheless, to me this is a great vulnerability and a step forward deeper into my own self -love. I am sure you have heard that saying "You have to love yourself first... once you learn to love yourself then you'll find someone right for you... or you have to be complete before you can find the real thing."

So, yes in some way it is true like this- but also those "failed" relationships were a huge success for your soul and for the universe as a whole because... they brought about more expansion! And, you learned something, didnt you? You inevitably learned from all of your relationships mainly because you believed they would make you happier, don't worry I'm in the same boat. But the ultimate relationship is with God. And that is beyond your wildest dreams, you cannot imagine all the love, the space, the sugar, the wisdom, and the discipline of being married to God, married to the universe at large. There is such a grace. It says first as a whisper without looking quite only at you, including Mr. Leo thee author, I have all the possible earrings including your favorite and I don't mind of you really LOVE EVERYONE.

I would like to pray that you may find the underlying reality of God in ALL relationships. And by the way if I haven't said this earlier, God is a word, a sound, it is also a concept, but it is also deeper and more real than that, that is what I truly am referring to when I say God. To truly know God you must be willing to change with God.

The nuns and the monks are all married to God, and I guess you could say all beings are their children, and it would be lovely if we all conducted ourselves as if that was the case. The only difference between the life of a purely religious, a nun or monk, and a regular run of the mill person is the vows. The nuns, the monks, have made promises to themselves and God, these promises include chastity, poverty, and obedience. I would say that is much more of an actual relationship than most marriages between a husband and wife.

This is why I am taking this spin on divine relationships. If you want to read about the things that many people have written about that is not my interest, my interest is to provide MY perspective in the hopes that it helps YOUR perspective, that is all. I could even say this; we are experiencing together as a writer and a reader or audience a divine relationship- there is certainly Truth in it and Truth behind it- isn't that something we are trying to get from relationships is that "what-is –behind-it?" I bet I am the genuine <u>article</u>- that's a writing pun that can mean whatever you want it to be about my dear friend of the soul – us having relations here.

And I want you to feel safe in my words and wisdom and Trust. The divine is something that can present itself between "two" different beings in divine relationships and that becomes the focus and the only way that is possible is through Trust alone- there is no real way sometimes without relationship we cannot always be alone or find "The Golden" inside our closed off place we remedy our closed off nature and venture forth into the Light of our shared world in its uncontrollable and unknown behaviors manifesting constantly through others- you can naturally begin to feel the humility in it, and that is always God's will.

When we return to our aloneness we are to simply achieve a goal of not hating those in which we shared relationship with and we can understand the divinity in ALL of it. This book is certainly helping us not hurting us- even though the beginning of the true path of healing can seem like it is hurting us because it is exposing the wound(s) for us to properly and eventually be healed- The presence of the Lord is never demeaning of our experience and we should adhere to that we need not inflate ourselves to fully enjoy life- I may have brought you into alignment alas' near how I relate with or of God through these direct, meaningful, and honest words. Nothing about the goodness of relationship is forced because it is focused correctly which is set aimed at the core of the being; the entire relationship and resonates there for all of time in the divine soul! - but there is not I could even say that is the mission statement of this entire book. A book I would like to mention is "Man's Eternal Quest" by Paramhansa Yogananda*. I see him as the yoga instructor for all Americans because he brought yoga to the west in the 1920's and it spread like wildfire. Yoganadaji was someone who mastered and continued to practice and teach the art of Kriya yoga. This form of yoga focuses on the spinal column; the sushumna, and is said to be the most direct way to God-realization, whether you realize God or not it is whole heartedly worth your while, even though I don't practice Kriya yoga. I practice Joe-ga… my own adaptation and inter-mixture of Hatha, Kundalini, and Yin Yoga, in which there is Pranayama.

Paramhansaji's lineage goes back to Babaji, the mahavatar who apparently still resides and reveals himself to devotees on the path of enlightenment in the Himalayas. It is said that if you repeat his name thrice he will surely appear. Ram ram. So, we are still talking about divine relationships right? Right. Divine is the relationship that you are in right now with these words, with these souls that I am mentioning for a very specific and direct reason because your soul is ready. Divine is the air you breathe. Divine is your inner and outer sight without which you would not know the world. These practices like Yoga are designed to essentially manifest endless joy.

Yoga can be used for the highest purposes but also you can see its benefits in every experience. The reason I believe that these Indian saints of old have a grip on me is because God wants to use them to help the world in this present age and time. All of them that I mention have the boundless understanding of perfect love and awareness. This is literally what America needs to move beyond our limited and now detrimental states of mind and into a more expansive one. To have a relationship with God is to have a relationship with all, and to have a relationship with one is to have a relationship with God as the one. Namaste.

Archangel Chamuel Bless us All the archangel of divine relationships.

The same sign Earth sign I was so in love with when I was certainly able-bodied and fiery with passion in a more obvious way being younger and yet not so confused as I could have been generally- I guess to be frank may the divinity present in one being in those relationships whether they happen or do not become dominant and a force of eventually unconditional Love- I am thankful for my experiences on thee Earth and proud of what choices I have made and where I have aimed my arrow of Life- my concise prayer is to give creedence to the blossoming Spirit which seems to be reckless yet is abundant and willing to be seen the root technically of all of them and the epitome of God's will in the form of free will- may it be excersized properly and may the relationships be made to bend toward the divine which is whole and complete for is born of perfection eternally! Amen.

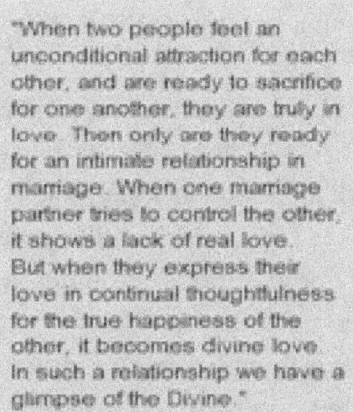

"When two people feel an unconditional attraction for each other, and are ready to sacrifice for one another, they are truly in love. Then only are they ready for an intimate relationship in marriage. When one marriage partner tries to control the other, it shows a lack of real love. But when they express their love in continual thoughtfulness for the true happiness of the other, it becomes divine love. In such a relationship we have a glimpse of the Divine."

Paramahansa Yogananda

Archangel Raphael

Archangel Michael

30
ANGELS AND SPIRITUAL GUIDES

What really is an angel? Is it the same as a spirit guide? Why is it important?

I will first answer the last question. It is important because we all need guidance and support on every level from God, which comes through angels and spiritual beings. Angels and spirit guides are messengers for God, we need them because they can embody God for us temporarily or maybe over our lifetime. This demystifies the divine and allows our minds to use a focal point and to carry out new necessary communication with these beings of God. I have heard many interesting things about angels; that they don't really have wings and are more of an ovoid shape of a specific frequency range of light.

I have heard that the line between highly evolved beings, like Extra-Terrestrials, and angels can be difficult to locate, meaning that you may be talking with an angel who is really an Arcturian or vice versa but that isn't too clear. Later in this book I will discuss ET's in its own right.

Angels are commonly known as beings of unconditional love and positive regard. They may or may not incarnate in physical form. The traditional belief of religious pastimes has been that there is a heaven in which angels live and sing. By the way they are typically referred to as Seraphim and Cherubim. They are sometimes sent to Earth to assist us who knows if there is really any distance from heaven to Earth? Also the typical belief is there is a guardian angel that we each have next to us. The most popular angels are the archangels. I have heard there are from 7 to 14 of these specific angels, it doesn't really matter if you are pure light "how many" of you there are, does it? But I enjoy the personification of light, so I will share what I know about these beings known as archangels.

There are at least 12 archangels and it is easily associated and remembered with the 12 signs of the Zodiac.

Archangels; each of them has a name and a purpose unto God. The most well known is Michael whose name means the one who is "like God". He is the protector and defender of Truth and resonates with the throat chakra.

He typically destroys demons for God when called upon and can also provide wisdom and guidance and can embolden and assist the growth of the divine masculine within humanity (and of course the divine feminine), which is the innate desire to protect and to serve and love in this way specifically. The next is Raphael; he is the one who is the "medicine of God".

Raphael is the healer Arch-angel, he can heal most anything with God's love and when God so designs it to be healed. Raphael is a great companion to have, his and all angels energies can be very subtle and go completely unnoticed but I think sometimes that is for the better because as long as we receive the love then all is well, but when we are meant to be more aware of angelic energy we will be (starting now I hope)…

Gabriel is the "power or Hero of God". He (angels *may* not have as clear gender lines as humans do we could say eh) is the messenger angel who came to visit Mary when she was going to be pregnant with Jesus, he apparently told her what to name him, so that is what I see as a very clear and specific message. It seems sometimes when we think of angels we think of a sometimes vague experience but this one with Mary was very clear and direct, which is great. This can be very intimidating because it is ALWAYS important… *

Just like all our families… and the root of it which is the God given impulse to exist and continue existing- the root of lasting Peace, that may be a few steps ahead because for us to come into coexistence with THAT TRUTH is what puts our fatherly and motherly feet on the path of actual Peace- it is logically the only to do so- we are like when people discuss being covered in the Blood of Christ and we don't even want to see the world through the blood piercing our eyesight and we feel, alone, just feel. We are not submitting to the difficulty but rather coming to grips with what we are and what we will become when we have children and that cannot be without a root and we are creators and the more proud of that the more we will know Peace- the goal is to find out what it is that we are putting up with that is not allowing more of the implied and inherent goodness to be more known in our lives ESPECIALLY in our children's lives that- root will carry on after "we" the parents pass on… generally toward heaven!

These above angels are the big three, I could compare them to the three tenors, Pavarotti, Domingo, and Carreras.* I believe that these angels cover all the bases but there are even more! I do apologize for my ignorance on the translation of the next Angels names, but I am sure we could find that on google. Next we have Ariel, she is the primordial nature angel and works specifically with and for the Earth and its greater good. I feel her as I type in my heart. Also each archangel resonates with a zodiac sign, Ariel is the Aries. The innocent character from "The Little Mermaid"* also had that name 'Ariel' she in growth was such a creature and a feeler, giver, potential healer, and beauty just as every single one of all of the humans are stuck with being- interesting huh. The simplicity of living on the Earth and being innocent inherently is triumphant and the glorious victory is in our becoming not just our appearing and dying eventually. Thus is the best possible reason to love and care for the Earth with Archangel Ariel.

There is Zadkiel, who I see as purple and works with communication on all levels- The joys of communication are immense and we have no choice but to be utterly overwhelmed by them even-though they are forever on our side- those waves of potential energy those wavelengths waiting in our lungs physiologically speaking. A great song I recall from my experience as an adult was a song by *Charles Ives called "Rememberance" It was about a Father being remembered by his offspring in such a profound and real way- that was not so upsetting but accurate and desired to be shared- the mutuality of the desire to share by the knower and the beholder is the birth of communication! The great way of Light is upon its path because it is our destiny to have growth through knowledge not just raw experience and this is not anything else but communication- it carries us on and we must continue civilly and that is our only way (forward even if we are to falter- and seemingly fail forever).

There is Sandalphon the archangel of song and music, who resonates with the sign of Pisces- the intuitive water sign. We all love water and sometimes even atheists seem to be enamored by the Creator I AM when in water- The presence of music and water are similar aren't they? They have a manner that is so poetic- in the sense that they are never separate from reality and are yet so forthcoming in ALL of the aspects that would utterly divorce any person(s) from it; from reality. The hospitals are filled or with music and poetry for those who are but everyone and not even forced upon is that sweet watery sounds like its very base the nature of water and how the songs of the ages are each like a ripple – see how they coalesce- remembering God's and its attribute of kindness yet foundation outside of time and space… like just one body of water.

Another one is archangel Chamuel, she is designed to assist those who are in love and in relationships (which is pretty much everyone, always or so we think). She is very wise and understanding in my experience and it is a comfort to know that there is an angel who is specific purpose is to assist with the sometimes most difficult aspect of our life.- Like any good Earth sign seems to do. The grace of specific beings are involved utterly with their single personality and the grace of God being (perfect) Love must abide by its own single way to come through and honor itself; by reverberating (forever) within the personality. So the grace for these divine relationships is a solid foundation and potentially stoic honesty- like the sign of Taurus; grounded, stable, respectful. Divinely feminine in its receptivity and supplement.

There is Archangel Uriel, who is seemingly my favorite for a reason. He is the archangel of books and literature! He is most likely very happy with my work thus far and will help me to continue on. He is often seen holding a tome. He will help those whose human purpose is aligned with divine purpose! The list goes on and on but that is where I will shift to discussing angels in a different light and then on to spiritual guides in general. Thee flaming passions of our soulful loins being able to manifest is the greatest gift we give to ourself. It promotes peace in all places and saves souls in perfect relevance by our own persons experience and everything else amiss- thus is the nature of reading. To be willing to know yourself is a justice to your soul eternally- and what a world to revel in that could be hell, we will never know, without Books!

We may like to believe we have two angels assigned to us, usually one female one male, I believe that the name of my guardian angel is Malachi and HE resonates with the Color purple. I feel that there is great Love in these very personal relationships and are essentially our reminder of our heavenly essence. Matt Kahn is someone who is very blatantly open about his angelic roots, which makes me overjoyed because in reality we all can feel a little angelic from time to time, Yay.

***Archangels to complete writing about are:

1.Nathaniel (career/work, transformation, manifestation and life purpose)

The fire sign of Sagittarius is this Archangel it is in everyone the fire (of devotion) to accomplish tasks. Even those who are almost paralyzed lovingly I say for those are care takers to understand them best and accomplish their own task of caretaking. The human being naturally allows for more expansion of consciousness through honest work and revelry which is a very Sagittarian thing to do- The denial of it is only a misunderstanding and is eventually everyone's business to use our life and choices to manifest growth (through experience). The Master healer's perspective on this is that healing comes from every aspect of life technically even when we are not looking for it- by living in alignment. The intellectual acceptance of this fact allows for more good vibes we say to be around- separate from perhaps intense healing workshops or even external gestures in that way. The logic of this is thus: The goodness exists as it is; some call it God, but the way in which we focus in Life allows it to flow to us; the best foundation possible for all work is this understanding.

At the very least it will raise our vibes and our self-esteem, which, as a teacher of children, is very much my business and my priority. So, how does all of this apply to us at this moment? Good question inquisitive mind! I say that we all could use some help, that's pretty much it. Angels are there literally for that exact reason for all eternity they just might be more on top of their game than the average therapist... Even they falter. The Spiritual Guidance perspective on this is the moment to moment experience is brought to its Truth when us beings are witnessing how we are really influencing our shared world permanently and other souls- by doing (honest) work. Simple.

On to spirit guides... Spiritual guides are a hugely popular topic in the present day age, also known as the "new" age even though Truth is eternal and is not subject to change and is paradoxically also new because Love is the ultimate Truth and is never boring. Spirit guides will only help you if you trust them. Plain and simple, trust. If you feel that you are not interested in them they will remain in the background but they will step up when and if you so choose. They, just like angels, can be seen as forms that link you to the divine reality, which is you and is your sovereign birthright, they are just beings who are devoted to serving the divine reality of God.

So, I feel that the spirit guides guidance system is very familiar to us so much so that we may take it for granted without fully appreciating it. The spirit guides may be actual ascended beings that once were in our position in a past life, which qualifies them to guide us. But once again, as with any relationship, trust is the lubrication; the oil in the engine, to put it into words. One of the main goals of spirit guides is to not be obnoxious for example, they will provide hints and clues for the greater good but they will not demand much of anything, because they respect us, and ultimately love and care for us.

It can be very endearing and sweet to get to know your spirit guides but try to remain unattached for the very wise reason of letting go of expectations on them and on God, essentially I am looking out for your peace of mind, and peace of soul, which I have been doing all my life by the way, Earth beings.

If you would like to continue down this specific path of esoteric self-discovery, because we are all One, including the spirit guides and angels, I recommend using the technology available to you can use many videos that can reveal more information to us within meditation and intention to connect with God through these beings as permission slips. Isn't it lovely to know that we are so clearly connected forever and ever to ALL the possible goodness in all existence- the epitome of it being the Archangels and Spirit Guides who are constant from time immemorial.

The reason I feel admiration and hope for the future of humanity with these angels and spiritual guides is because they do not contribute to the suffering but rather open us to a more wise and relaxed way of conducting ourselves and navigating the sometimes difficult life on Earth. The angels and spirits guides are not coming from or are restricted to one dogmatic system but rather are encouraging us to broaden our outlook on the divinity of all reality. Ram Ram. There is no restricting energy in them at all but a exemplifying of goodness and invitation toward Trust- inherently. Please do seek a relationship personally (with God) through the angels and Spiritual Guides. I am one of them.

LOG OF MEDIA * authors website (www.joevertino.org)

Look at all the potential for healing with these hands of diversity's point!

31
DIFFERENT RELIGIONS AND THEIR PURPOSE FOR OUR FUTURE

I have been a seeker of the Truth my entire lifetime. My heart can be explained in one experience when I was younger; I would sit in my bedroom for long periods of time and do nothing physically; to me this was meditation and I felt very peaceful and happy to do this. I believe that this is my core and is what I aim to teach to whomever- because it was not an action-based activity meaning attempting to meet a demand in myself but yet in the lack of that presence I was content.

As I aged I began to perceive somewhat differently, though the heart remains the same. My mind would fixate on sermons on Sunday and I would ask my Mom about them several nights later on. I would contemplate and it came naturally for me.

As I grew and my mind considered more perspectives I explored philosophy, the possible absence of God, nihilism, and eventually returned to God and now I seek God first and religion second with every gesture of my life- like a swinging arm down a familiar alleyway in which you know you won't hit anything. This seems to be the step forward. The argument I will assert in this entry is the complimentary nature of ALL religions. That no ONE religion is "thee" one but all can be seen and used by God or the universe for its own divinity but do not be adverse to God using one religion deeply to open your heart for the great purpose of divinity and wisdom.

> In all respect like God can give rise to newly pubescent male's erection and the lure of it upon the soul with a movement of the mind toward a specific solidified consciousness we can label a religion for the sake of language's victory and not Spiritual pursuits loss, I declare.

I admire from a far all things as a True Buddhist and it is easier to admire perhaps religion(s). I am made to perceive and that which does strike at that must be not ignored in its or rather my process of self- mastery for the well-being of all souls- so as to prosper the world in which we will live. The general vantage point of consciousness is always that place in oneself- but I do speak about and from my own proud personal experience in this writing(s).

The mention of a name is involved in religion generally globally, uh, this is a separate declared at least one being throughout them all. It can be known that the point of Life inside or outside of "anything" including religion or ideas is to grow, something simple and irrevocable (?) irremoveable! Like a FETUS! The general impetus for these different and/or differing religions is the second half of our chapter; the purpose for our future which is all ours, and we are first and foremost a witness who naturally does not wish pain on anything; innocence. The complications that are preferable in Life are wholeheartedly "part" of the individuation process an inseparable aspect of our being unlike religion. Yet we can grow to see how this Truth of our core is leading us into the qualities of religion.

*From the Bible: "For the fruit of the Spirit is Love, Joy, Peace, patience, kindness, goodness, faithfulness, gentleness, self-control, for such there is no law." From Galatians 5: 22-23 new Testament (NIV) Even anarchists would be a smiling- on their motorcycles "from hell" – there a TV show, I am sure. The fellowship wound in a soul is so immense and we can run into so much turmoil in this lifetime and as a good Character, an author, I wish you to know that about Life. Nothing to say about convincing but my HEART brims with healing wisdom for you- and it is this; that just knowing that our divine need and craving for fellowship is attempting to be met in all the groups we could ever be involved with and certainly with will never be in jest unlike some of the labels of the groups. The manifestation of this reading is only Universal and personal Truth that is appearing…

For example, I often say how the Catholic Church should become flooded with yogic awareness. I actually believe in all seriousness that a well-disciplined yogi who has transcended enough of the lower ego energies would be a lifesaver for these struggling Priests. The only thing that would be necessary for these Priests to move forward with the Lord in this endeavor would be an opening of the mind for the greater good of the Earth – essentially, a lot of humility and a reverence for these soul seekers from a different land. At this point I am most heavily influenced by Hinduism for the exact reason that the Indian saints understand an underlying reality that is transcendent and is necessary for this exact moment in the evolution of all of humanity.

They have quietly held this Truth in their hearts and I am honored to be a mouthpiece for their divine wisdom in deep humbleness. The most popular prayer in my heart now is "Ram ram", which translates as God's Love. I enjoy this prayer because it can be used to cut through the illusion and give full mind focus onto God at any time anywhere.

The main purpose of religion is to bring one into the heart. Drunvalo Melchizedek and Jesus point at the heart in their portraits, Jesus is known as the sacred heart and Drunvalo's is known as the Illuminated heart. *

It has been made very obvious that there is something crucial and important in there. The Yogis in their ancient searchings saw that all the universe(s) exists within this heart. I am sure I could find several paintings from all the major world religions that come to some indication of the blessed Heart center.

The other spiritual paths I am enjoying exploring are ones that are exciting to me and my soul's growth. I see all of them with Love. Taoism is fun, I have done my research in regards to this and have become spiritually friendly with Lao Tzu.* The story of Lao Tzu is he was a sage of ancient china and was exposed to the culture there, he did less seeking and more finding of the Truth. He was the founder and actualizer of the "Tao" in taoism, which has become popular all around the globe in this present day with or without his consent after his death!

The most important and revealing story of Lao Tzu is this; he was known all throughout the great land of China and in his old age he was planning on leaving China for good but as he was leaving he encountered a special saint in the form of a Chinese guard, this guard pleaded with him to write down his teachings in a book and was successful. This man, Lao Tzu, lived in such a way that he was one with the Truth of the Tao, which can be understood in the opening sentiment of his book "The Tao te Ching" *- LOG OF MEDIA "The tao that can be spoken is not the eternal tao."

You can hear why he didn't on his own accord write anything down but did after he felt the heart of the guard at the gate of China, his motherland, asking for assistance for future spiritual seekers. What a blessing. Thank you Lord, amen.

The reason my perspective seems to disturb people is because we have put so much effort in separating the religions and I am here to destroy that. And I am here to stand in the Oneness of God reality. Wouldn't you rather be friends with all? The eastern religions possess much less judgment towards the mind because they do not as easily externalize their thoughts meaning they do not project them outward but keep them inside their own mind.

This can be as a two-edged sword but the reason this encourages peace for westerners is because they, the eastern practitioners, actually have a faith in reality that allows them to be somewhat detached from needing to influence people, places, and things in regards to their own well-being. For example, a true Buddhist will be much more comfortable sitting next to someone who is in pain than most westerners.

The reason for this is because they practice detachment. The extreme example of this is delineated in a picture that captured a Buddhist monk who was well aware that an elderly man had just passed away while sitting on a bench in a public place and he kindly took the corpses hand and held up his other hand to his chest and prayed for the man's spiritual repose in the afterlife, how present and accepting, full of grace and mindfulness.

Yes, there is compassion but there is also a sense of detachment from forcing things to become different for their own comfort. Once again, the grace in all of this is YOU, in the now, the person who is so open minded to read this and consider what I am asserting. That God created all religions to bring wisdom to the Earth not to have us quarrel like squirrels over the same nut.

There are endless beauties to be discovered throughout the richness of the religions that developed on Earth, but once you get tired you can find some more satisfying and lasting answers with more simple and laidback teachers. One that comes to mind now is named Mooji. I know his lineage, a lineage is a line of masters and students who later became masters to teach more students, it is kind of like an infinite loop that, to me, is quite beautifully represents the circle of Life and of God's heart, moving from darkness to Light, from ignorance to enlightenment with grace in every breath that is contagious from one person to another. Ramana maharshi taught Papaji and Papaji taught Mooji.

So, in deep reverence and respect and an all-encompassing Love for all beings and hope for their liberation, Mooji's lineage can be seen quite obviously in his satsang (his homilies) with Ramana Maharshi and Papaji present in images near to where Mooji sits. These satsangs last usually an hour and a half to three hours in length and are readily accessible on youtube.com.

Jesus is wildly popular today on the Earth but he is relatively modern compared to the spirituality that has been going on in foreign lands and everywhere for eons of time, or yugas as the Yogis come to understand it. This perception of time provides the Indian culture with much more ease in everyday life and less stress, which westerners could adopt, as we can all agree America is stressed! Make some friends with foreigners, you will not be disappointed, keep an open heart around them and enjoy them deeply. Be willing to learn from them and share with them you, as well. I believe this is God's will for us to come together as the Beatles said.

So, the primary ability for any sage is their deep love and comfort within the empty silence because this is a return to the blank page and when we have misused our free will to create things we no longer wish to continue we must scrap them and return to the first step.

The first eternal step is the silent awareness of God and the purity of the mind. When we are born and grow we have a mind that is unique and we don't feel compelled or at least shouldn't feel so compelled to quickly adopt a belief system to "save us" from whatever we have been conned into believing is "wrong" with us.

There are, of course, all the silly religions that are meant to be a satire of the traditional more serious ones like the flying spaghetti monster, which is used in arguments by atheists to convey a philosophical logical perspective on God saying it is just the same as a flying spaghetti monster meaning it can't be disproven that there is a flying spaghetti monster somewhere in existence and they say that there is a similar logic to the existence or "proof" of God. I believe that the attempt to prove God would do some damage to the unique experience of discovering God through more than just your mind's left hemisphere.

There is no proof that "silence" exists but how can we argue against it? I don't know. But all I do know is that we have to rest sometime and I choose to rest in the full awareness of unconditional Love, which is God itself and

Reiki vibes of Zen which is my peace and home vibration. So, the important issue in this one passage is … tradition! I feel the love for tradition but I do not aim to offend. I believe that tradition is based on deep respect and honor and that's it! If we uphold these two values we should be good when encountering deep tradition, but as you well know by now I am into what is deeper. Tradition is sometimes beautiful and sometimes ugly.

The reason for this can be understood for a simple reason when we use tradition to cover our fear we become ugly and when we use it with the Truth of Love we look beautiful. But in reality beauty is in the eye of the beholder. See my passage on Beauty for more words on this.

The other alternative religions from my perspective are shamanic paths, druidism, paganism, as well as voodoo and Santeria. These religions can be very confusing for most people who are rooted in different more subtle cultures like North America. But you can experience a wild perspective if you get so lucky and feel so inclined on a soul level. In foreign lands there are ways of relating to the spiritual realities that are quite loud, agitating, and penetrating to our mind if we allow it to be so.

These practices are not so well known to me in this particular lifetime but instead of the typical fear of miscommunication if I was to be present in a shamanic ceremony somewhere across the oceans I would find a deep space of Love in my heart for them and their lifestyle. The common threads penetrate deeper I promise. My favorite means of practicing shamanism is music the way Bobby Mcferrin does, he is elderly now, thank you a deep bow to you. The common threads are creativity, food, comfort, affection and music. VIDEO LOG OF MEDIA * Video of him singing a song to a great crowd.

*The Dalai Lama says his religion is kindness, and we all need kindness. Here in Buffalo the most true part of it is that it truly is the city of good neighbors and that goes a long way! The Dalai Lama also said that the common thread for all beings is that we "Seek out happiness and wish to avoid suffering." This applies to all beings not just those with reason and logic of their own but even the bugs, the grass, the trees, and the sea lions swimming the seas, and all the humans.

So, to conclude the main point here is that we will find a deeper sense of happiness and joy when we are willing to be yourself regardless… regardless of the culture, the language, the ceremony or their specific traditions that may or may not be wise to perpetuate for our future. I believe in real Love. Ram ram. I don't know how to stop the pain you may endure in this life but I do know that there is kindness found wherever you open your heart. And I know in my heart that the great Truth of love will guide you to where you are most needed and most comforted. Happy healing.

Truth appearing in front of our eyes because true Love is never far from the Truth. Isn't it nice knowing we are all on the same side as far as needing healing and that there are means to that end that are ultimate and conclusive- the best being the tradition of Reiki? As we well know we are meant to give way to more friendship and less adversity which comes from the lack of awareness even if just a little bit and to expand rather than contract our entire life. Now we can say and perhaps see easily how being aware and also being honest with yourself helps- it helps our future as a Species and also- now we can understand that like an armor of consciousness we are stabilizing and if we do this; incorporate this, we can call it practice and lifestyle which are purely religious terms not many can argue that like even from afar like as a young child who can walk through a library full of important ideas obviously whilst not entertaining any of them but fully experiencing their own. Religion is #1 spot in these terms to make a clear point of progress for our future- Our collective understanding of practice and lifestyle is that Religion is superior to other "things" in its category.

Like other modalities of exercising our free will. These are others in that category in which practice and lifestyle are appropriate terms in all seriousness. The "religious" in combination to the nature of being human is not superseded. So, the use of free will with this is the most powerful. The point is already made universally but we can hear its words: So, It is that even if someone was to be instructed and masterful at another modality- the ecstasy that comes from both understanding the use of free will in all (sincere) practice and lifestyle at its peak or zenith is now a "religious" thing.

People who have personal religious experiences are mandated to follow a new Path after their inescapable recognition that doesn't negotiate but even comes over the neighbor's fence of different modalities – because religion is not a quarrelsome thing- this is one Universal reason why Religion in all its misunderstanding is unimpeded on and on it goes unlike other things that we could SEE or SAY IS COMPETITIVE WITH IT- hopefully not on and on!

The point to be clear is that religion being misunderstood and it is not good for us and our future- it is guaranteed detrimental. And the core of children, to use a serious word, is curiousity which implies purpose and as we realize we cannot all explore outer space or be the president one day and have sex with everybody the next day etc. on and on with the examples… We begin to hopefully retain this predominantly our innocence which is a purposeful desire to REALIZE; which is the core of CURIOUSITY. So, religion is fundamental in the ultimate practical sense alone and houses the natural human in a safe place to take serious themselves and the journey ahead which inevitably includes "not-knowing" which just like religion inherently cannot be superseded! I find this very un-funny and sincerely hopeful. Religion is always supportive and that our time with God can be a conscious objective and external experience- and it is good and brings out a special clarity and mystery "in" us. Something that we can end with is that it ultimately has an individual base and can be UTILIZED- It is not wrong to think in those terms. In context of our chapter title we are thinking about how it is useful already! So, my hope is that these words have provided you with enough Truth on what religion really is that it can manifest naturally in and around you in our shared world without cause for terror- and just as religion is always exercised through our free choice(s) so is the things that are destructive that can never be religious even if they are very confusing and criminal.

So, how has this helped you? Have you gained a more powerful grip on "your" head? That is the only thing God is interested in my dear friend. The unfortunate circumstances of Life may you let them give way to God's immense non-understandable will! As we have tried over and over again up to this point to succeed at life by bringing in new people, places, and things! We are not really a failure or are we really even failing but we are destined for greatness by way of relief alone. It is such an honor to be used by the Lord to be welcoming of Life everyday and how that becomes of me is these words to you, it is that simple! The way God sees the Universe is never our business but the way God loves is always and forever our business- and it is always a personal experience with it- thus "Different Religions and their purpose for our future."

The Dalai Lama – Buddhist mastery figure- stable in Compassion- to preach (mentioned throughout the book) age of at least 90

32
HEALING

The big one! It goes without saying; healing is one of the most, if not the most, important topics of our age because everything is either going towards healing or going away from it. The power of Love is to neutralize the ego enough that it can be still and then the soul or the higher-self mind can choose to generate love and healing for itself and others. The healing energy I am most familiar with is Reiki. On a soul level, I believe that Reiki has the capacity to heal anything and everything imaginable because even though it is dramatically simple and subtle it, for that very reason, is capable of healing all of the chaos and painful trauma we experience AND I truly believe that Reiki is the white light of God available throughout time and space because it is prior to both.

For example, when I was a child I had night terrors, I would sit up straight in my bed and with eyes wide open would cry big sloppy tears.

But I would still not wake up. My parents would rush to my room and my Mom would hold tight onto my body. I believe that the blankness of Reiki is healing. Instead of demanding anything from your mind, your heart, your body, your spirit, and/or your soul Reiki simply does what it does, and goes where it is most needed naturally. You do not have to believe anything about it, you do not have to say any prayers to make it work properly, from the receiving end, and you do not have to do much of anything or even stop much of anything to be healed by a Reiki healer.

My Reiki journey began many lifetimes ago. In this life I went to a psychic, a very pleasant one, I was told that I would do hands on energetic healing work. Some time later I came across another Psychic and she said "I see the word Teacher written across your forehead." a Reiki level 1 course and I immediately felt a very obvious calling from my heart center to explore this further. I have never felt anything quite like that. I followed my heart, which as I said could not have been more obvious if GOD smacked me in the face, and I went into the institution and registered for the class.

I now, several years later, have acquired the title and certification of a Reiki master teacher. This qualifies me, with a deep bow to the Reiki lineage branching out from eternity through the past *Zen monk Dr. Mikao Usui, who is the founder of the Usui Reiki School and lineage, to give full healing sessions to clients, to myself, and to teach the art of Reiki healing work, to continue the lineage. I also am certified through another teacher to work on animals, thank you ma'am for teaching and guiding me. It was also stated in the psychic reading that I would work with my partner, I hope that comes true someday.

Moving on… there are so many modalities and single perspectives on healing that it can be overwhelming to me somedays. But, when you find one that works then remember that. My second choice for healing is general prayer. I have a page on facebook entitled "Healing Prayers".

 On this page I essentially type out a paragraph long prayer from my heart, spontaneously, completely based on the energy flowing in that moment, there are no repeated prayers on my prayer page. I believe this is important and useful to people in reference to healing and guidance because I feel that the precision of Love is what heals us. So, when someone decides to read these prayers the vibration that God and I are One can be felt and can rapidly unravel much of the sufferings.

This is an example of one:

Lord God, I thank you for this day and the night that follows and for all the experiences held within. I thank you for this Earth and all its wonders. I thank you for all the opportunity you give to us and I pray that for those who do not have the same opportunity that we can somehow give to them what they need. I pray those who are most fortunate can also become the most giving and generous. I pray that the wisdom of the sages can be made easily understandable. I pray we can grasp the reality of your LOVE and can find harmony, balance, and equilibrium within it. In the name of the Great Spirit, Amen.

When these prayers are received with great trust they have great power to shift energies within and around you for the greater benefit of all beings. Because there is only One heart in existence, when you pray from that place you are immediately connected to every other being, not just on earth, but in the cosmos. This is why an earnest prayer avails much because it comes from a place of innocence and can bring someone back to that place. This is what Jesus meant when he said "only those who are like little children may enter the kingdom of heaven." *The kingdom of heaven may very well be your own divine heart.

As you may remember from earlier words in this book I believe that the greatest healing of all is the liberation of the soul. What I mean is moksha or transcendent enlightenment. The reason this is the most powerful is because it directly prevents suffering from being perpetuated needlessly. The reason is because when we surrender the mechanism that is causing the pain the pain disappears. The ego is that. But in addition the ego cannot push itself off the cliff and into the sky. Only God is capable. And those who whole-heartedly live for God are destined for the great awakening of that within them and around them. The hope in all of this is that the actual reality is pure, simple and direct. This should provide some relief when we become tired of suffering.

I have often watched as the guru would speak and I would feel the place of wisdom and Truth and emptiness within them and see the difference of the place where the student is located. On One beautiful level you could say the student or seeker is in the heart of the guru and of God but they just don't know it yet.

The guru is not trying to change things; the guru is both the change, the things that are changing, and the primary awareness. The scary awesome part of this all is that the student is not in control. And the guru is only given control when they have relinquished their own desire for control. This healing is enlightenment, which I would like to mention, can also be transmitted through Reiki. The more conventional method or nomenclature is shakktipat, which is an ancient label for the guru consciously allowing positive healing love waves whether broad or narrow, wide, or focused, to be sent to the student(s) through them because The divine is real and needs to be at work- when souls are in its wake- but we are responsible for putting ourself there and also can accept grace.

> Being open to Grace is a great way to live your (entire) life… out. If you know rather than anything else or otherwise attempts to improve yourself – this knowledge you cling to will also want to cling to you- and then you are constantly connecting to God; and God is the All in All.

Spiritual exercises also have great healing power. Yoga, Tai Chi, combined with meditation can move the soul to create life anew which essentially is the root of healing and a conscious decision to change for the good of all. I believe that in the present age it is very important that the yogis (those who practice yoga) understand that Yoga is half spiritual and half corporeal. The Americans seem to focus on the physical more. This is still better than not doing the exercise at all, perhaps, but you are actually missing the point, you are doing exercise, not Yoga. Yoga means "union... with God"... sometimes I like to call it Yo-God!

The reason this is important is for the same reason when the Buddhist Tibetan monks chant Om, or Aum... they emphasize the last consonant, mmm. The reason, spiritually, for this is cleansing and uplifting and releasing the pain upward toward the central sun, galactic center, or the Buddha field. This is necessary for healing. Healing, like I said, will happen regardless, the only decision you have to make is will you work with it willingly and consciously? I hope so, because I don't want you to suffer anymore. The manner of Life is the same with us and with itself the grass- The shoots go forward into our shared world by way of like a vacuum in the sky- what a beautiful world being created over and over gain by each new thing- its contents. WE are the same an example like when we do Yoga we are arching ourself like a bow, like a frog, and providing awareness alone. Then as we shed our skin like the snake which takes ethical movement to do so- meaning we have to not harm ourself or stir into commotion unnecessary sufferings- but yet we can live, move, and have our being. Healing is an investment that has already been set up before we were born!

The inclination toward it is a clear SELF LOVING ACT- AND FURTHER it is an act that has no recourse for once it has dawned- like the the newest Sun, but still you know of a sun and what it's like- because that real(est) love has been latent and we have been born into it- its existence was complimentary to our own- and was like a consciousness we might access in this lifetime- that is what true healing is like. The most real possible grace is that OPTION TO BE HEALED- This is only if you choose it (in this lifetime). The omnipotence of God cannot force our "soul" to heal and it cannot "destroy" it. Because it is never right and God is rightness and is self-sustaining, like Noah's Ark. It sees and brings us up higher like Yogic practice to a realer yet more subtle plain sight; eventually attaining Nirvana!

The other mode of healing linked to prayer is mantra or prayer by rote memory/repetition. Mantra is used to bring the mind towards divinity and the purpose of it is to move through good concentration as a first step with the goal of full silent sitting or meditation in emptiness. How this works is the mind is like a teenager that needs some structure in its life so it can grow properly and not destroy everything in its path. The mind has IMMENSE potential and should be respected as such, it is not "bad" it is divine when we realize WE are divine. This first step of concentration is a bit overrated for me but if you feel it in your heart then go for it, repeat that mantra preferably in a sing song fashion.

The idea here is would you rather have a beautiful prayer in your mind or random, somewhat painful thoughts? Prayer is a good choice. The good thoughts come later on. It is much better to be addicted to mantra than most anything else from a societal standpoint. You actually should start to feel a sense of ease when praying, that is the good stuff. I include mantra as prayer here. My favorite is the Hindu or Sanskrit prayers around Ram mainly because it is set to beautiful music… Krishna Das Krishna Das! Jai. Ram ram. So, the next step of an alternative route is sitting, that's it… it's not much of a practice is it. But you must understand for someone like myself this can be very joyful. When I was a child this is what I would do for fun! This is the most pleasant way to achieve nirvana. When you open your heart and love pours out and takes over the whole existence including you and all that you are -you get it.

Anyways, the biggest ritual if I could use that word here is a chronic need and soul-filling relationship with the entire surrender process, from beginning to completion.

Surrender should get its own chapter in my book! To give up the pointless is what it is to surrender fully. It's like when things just happen, you aren't involved in them changing. This is surrender. Moving beyond and into the experience, it is always better to see things from the side of curiosity rather than being demanding. The reason this is disturbing to the ego is because it is the absence of it. The real grace is all that exists.

Apparently my soul felt like being totally gnarly in this life because I have more experiences of surrender than I can count on my hands and toes. It is even OK, if it's not OK. This is the weird part- that I cannot describe what it means to "allow" properly but the freedom from choice can be so nice. Real Love is all that there is yet we often miss it. The surrender is returning to our innocent state. This state is primary and is our home. It is the answer to all our prayers and paradoxically the place they come out of. Silly, I know, but beautiful.

> The greatest decision ever made is when a person decides they would rather be Love than anything else.

There is something called charismatic healing. A priest who has apparently transmuted enough of his lower energies can engage with the energy body of another person. In the Christian and Catholic tradition one Priest I am fond of is Father Richard Mcalear *. I have shaken his holy hand and attended two of his healing masses and enjoyed his book "The Power of Healing Prayer". The people walk up and they receive the Holy Spirit from him and his team and he uses the traditional oil and uses his thumb to mark the sign of the cross upon the brow, also known as the third eye point. Jesus said "If your eye be single, your body will be full of LIGHT." Quote from the Holy Bible; New Testament Matthew 6: 22 - There is a video of him in the LOG OF MEDIA. *

The reason this is important is because I can make a case against the ignorance and connect the dots within the Christian mind structure that Jesus was perhaps enlightened and he knew full well about the energy body. Another scripture passage to this point is when "Moses went into the desert to raise up the serpent [of light]". * This to me is very obviously about the Kundalini awareness that flows up the spinal column, also known as the sushumna, and that Moses was also well versed in the ancient art of chakra work. This can be very humbling to a Christian and instead of them claiming to know everything, they may enjoy listening for a while to a different yet beautiful perspective on the background of the prophets in their own chosen religion. Mother Mary and the disciples were seen with flames of spirit above their heads, which is another indication of the shakti energy at play in the human energy body.

So, how does this relate to healing you may think to yourself? Well, the reason is because the chakra points and the awareness of the glory of God does not depend on a belief system. It is a universal experience of Truth that can be a great unifying commonality for all. Remember how I mentioned earlier that you are either moving towards healing or away from healing? You can choose to find the mental relief in the point I am making and the argument I am asserting; that would be healing for the Earth and humanity because it would bring us together as One. Negative energy is based on segregation and perpetuating isolating thought patterns, positive energy is based in the deeper Truth of Oneness, common goals, excitement, joy, growth, enlightenment, healing, and unconditional Love. Do you believe that God created us as equal? Do you believe that God created us and designed us to develop and grow? If, so you can use the energy body and chakra points to achieve this just as the ascended masters did, which JESUS * is one of. Something you may like to research is the Great White Brotherhood and all of the lovely people and saints like Saint Germain and Djwhal Khul, and the chohans of the 7 rays of rainbow awareness, love, and light. I would seriously consider questioning the mind structure of anyone who feels that having a heavenly host of spiritual masters to commune with is wrong. Enough said.

The next thing in this healing installment is the violet flame of transmutation.

The ascended masters are related to this topic but the beckoning of this spiritual power transcends religious boundaries I know this for a fact because in the book "The Human Aura" * by Kuthumi, and Djwhal Khul the violet flame is used to heal by both the Buddhist masters and ascended masters of different faith's despite their varied cultural and religious backgrounds. The violet flame is so named because it is purple, which is the highest vibrational color in the humanly visible spectrum. It is quite simple how this works, the violet flame transmutes all the lower energies into the highest, which is violet. The chakra system is based on the rainbow, the rainbow is based on white light, also known as the light of God or of creation, this Light when refracted through a prism as seen with a clear master quartz crystal becomes a rainbow.

The root chakra; red, the sacral chakra; orange, the solar plexus chakra; yellow, the heart center; green, the throat chakra; light blue, the third eye center; indigo, and the crown chakra; violet, white or gold. Make sense? The lower ego energies are healed by the higher because as we grow we gain more wisdom, that is why it is important to listen to our elders with respect and honor for them, all the experiences we have are on their way to God's heart moving through our crown chakra to be used by the soul for growth in alignment with divine purpose. Ram ram. In all honesty, healing coming from this book does not end or begin within this installment, all of the words I say and write are intended for healing purposes.

Archangel Raphael bless us all.

33
SPIRITUAL ENTITIES AND HOW THEY MAY MATTER TO YOU

We have heard so much stuff about demons and angels. We have seen movies like* "The Exorcist" and the shows like "Touched by an Angel". Why is it important? The basic reason is it can be really annoying. If you have a demon bothering you then you are going to want it to stop. But, to be fair if there was an angel who was bothering you may also want them to stop. So, the point of this post is peace of mind, peace of soul. Sometimes it can be fun to destroy what is bothering you like spiritual warfare, Ram! Other times it can be used for your soul growth to leave it alone. To discuss this second point I would like to mention two very interesting beings. One is alive, one is dead. * St. Padre Pio was a stigmatic priest, meaning he seemed to bare the wounds of Christ spontaneously. He was holy and was attacked by demons regularly. This was used to foster a deeper connection with God because the demons can only attack what is illusory within us and around us to some degree. So, for him, St. Padre Pio, it was used to focus him and to transcend the corporeal attachments to comfort and to seek respite in God alone rather than temporary things bound to change. Another person who is very close to my heart is Steven Gray also known as Adyashanti.

He does not discuss spiritual warfare but the one anecdote that is relevant here is his story of his dog, being distracted, and meditating alone. He had a meditation hut in his parent's backyard when he was younger and his dog would join him outside for this activity. He sat down in the hut alone one day and the dog decided to circumvent the hut, but every time the dog passed by a section of the hut his body would scrape and this made it nearly impossible to meditate. This is related in the sense of annoyance. Instead of putting the dog inside the house he chose to use this experience for his soul growth and surrender into enlightened awareness and proper detachment from circumstances which breeds great freedom and inherent and blissful peace.

I am a firm believer that real peace is more useful than fighting the sometimes questionable spiritual energies. For example, what if you get enlightened first and then realize you actually don't care enough to try to destroy the bad vibes. In reality Love is the only thing that can tame the beast. One of many experiences with blatantly malicious vibes I have had is as follows: I was in a dream state and I saw an entity that was very uncomfortable for some reason it was surrounding my vision with red and was seemingly aware it was doing this, but something happened all of the sudden in which this light blue cloud of Love took over the entire view. This is why in my deepest state I realize we are in fact all Love. Instead of thinking of a plan or trying to process what was going on and the obvious fear present with this being all I felt was pure unconditional Love and it seemed to end. Apparently I learned what I needed to learn very quickly in this case. I have had many experiences with what seems like demons whether in dreams or in waking life. I do have some validation from these, one being the eyes.

I noticed some consistency, which, as you can confer from a scientific perspective, is an indication of considerable evidence pointing at some possible truth, in this case the existence of actual demons. To me this is intriguing, I don't have much of an ego so that isn't in my mind confusing my experience, if I encounter a demon I would take all the wisdom and knowledge I could from that experience and use it for my soul's growth whether I fight and destroy that demon returning it to God or source or whether I let it play out naturally. Either way it is intriguing and cures experience and, in reality, I bet most people if not all have had some experiences already with malicious entities, the reason I say this is because Earth is a very interesting and intense place to learn on.

With this being said, the clear difference to detect a demonic presence is first of all the feeling you get in your heart chakra. The next step is resonating consciously with the Light of God and seeing FROM and AS that LIGHT. In this place you are safe and can feel God's love no matter what this entity seems to be up to. You can see the difference between the light and the dark and see that light is direct and clear information and darkness is an intent to confuse and to abuse the truth, twisting it into its own gain at the expense of others well-being. Something I noticed is that whenever a situation is new I seem to revert back to the blank slate awareness and I become a Tibetan Buddhist for a second, I notice that I resonate only with the sound of "OM" and my mind becomes blank. This is useful because then you remain neutral and from that place you are not swayed into something else without your own choice from neutral mind space.

I once got a compliment that was so grand from a Felician nun. She said that I had a heart that was after Jesus's heart and that my mind was like an eastern one or more Buddhist in its nature." The reason this compliment was so pleasing to me is because it is true. The reason this is important to you reading this is because I seem to be balanced. And most people seem to still be working on this balance point within them. The courage to face anything including termination of existence is the heart and the mind that does not busy itself unnecessarily and that is tranquil. This is how God made me and I am well pleased. I aim to share this with you through this book- the open mind is necessary the judging mind is not.

To become more Zen you can relax in any experience. Imagine the last time you were super agitated and now go into that state and relax… completely. That is the power of Zen. You can find peace anywhere and everywhere, this Zen is pleasant because it is not tied to a belief system or a prayer or an invocation. The Zen is actually just the natural state. And you realize that you are actually quite safe and that experiences are more for entertainment and less for business and stress.

I assume the reason Zen came into this post is because it is what I would hope and prefer would be the case for you. I know how the mind works, and I also know how Zen feels. Choose Zen. Be happy no matter what happens. And just in case you are questioning the ethics of Zen, it doesn't have ethics besides what the present moment contains inherently. Anything unnecessary is gone. But the best part of Zen is that it is joyful and it is sorrowful and it is you and it is me. It is the deeper you and me that is eternal and aware of ALL. That is love.

But if there is a demon in your face don't be afraid of it. Tell it to go away. If it continues you can brighten the light within and see through God's heart and watch as God takes care of it all. Miracles occur. But also God may want you to pray for its removal. Don't hesitate if you feel like doing so. The rosary is a very powerful prayer only because Mother Mary is very powerful because she and God are One in all things. And she is not afraid of the things. She is not afraid of any demon and is very wise and ultimately loving. I'll have you understand that it is not about anything but discernment and that if God is (on the side of) Light and Light is at its core information then it is fundamentally that if you know, then you can decipher and discern- this is what holiness must be so close to and it is always holy to destroy what is evil. This is also why demons create confusion- but really it is us who are confused because we are not allowing ourself a true security. Something that I would like to reveal to you here is my experience with an exorcist that is countercultural. We, being the general public, only have the media to go off of in regards to demons and the priests that deal with them. The one time I met an actual exorcist he was the most gentle and soft-spoken man you could ever imagine. Why is this? I say because REAL power requires the lightest touch. The movies we see like *"The exorcism of Emily Rose" are based on an overly extreme concept; the real deal does not require screams and yells of bible verses during windstorms in barns while a poor lady is tied down with ropes.

And if that ever does go on in reality I would LOVE to attend. But, my point of this is that demons are nothing to worry about and if you are interested in the difference between the LIGHT and the DARK you can use your heart to discover some truths. For one you manifested this book! That's a great step forward. God doesn't make mistakes and there is a reason you have chosen or been chosen to read and perhaps study these words and there is a reason I am thrilled to write them for you.

God wastes NO experience. God would not give you an experience that wasn't serving a purely loving and divine purpose, ultimately. But do not overlook the simplicity of God and the heart of God to use any experience to deepen the uniqueness of his or her Love for us.

Ultimately it seems that is what God wants for us to realize. And the connection between spiritual paths and God's Love is that the LOVE is the motivation and the supplier of energy UPON the path that we have chosen to seek God out on. In the next section I will be discussing devotion and this is directly related to this divine relationship.

P.s. Look for wisdom in the experience, always.

Hanuman – Hindu deity (what a lovely color scheme)

34
DEVOTION

Devotion was created by God to return his souls unto himself. We are truly never separate from God but we can be so involved with certain affairs that we forget our Lord and his perfect Love- devotion is the remedy. What does it mean to be devoted? It requires a subject and an object doesn't it? The devotee and the beloved/the object of devotion. So, in the simplest case - a) the soul who may or may not be lost and b) God as the ultimate reality.

This is the case until you attain nirvana, meaning you and the divine perfection become One from all sides. The reason I say "from all sides" is because we may sometimes forget we are never separate from God but we also know that God always is fully aware that we are One, in the deepest sense, with her. But when all sides have been made aware of this- that is nirvana.

Now to make some more sense here and play out a description of some simple yet foundational steps of the spiritual process, which is not as much of a collection of anything but a removal of distraction. When all has been removed you and the reality either exist together or in the nothingness you can say there is perfect unity. This is why a sage said "My heart tells me I am everything, my wisdom tells me I am nothing, between these two my life flows…" (Nisargadatta Maharaj). So, in some simple words I would like to connect some dots. The first step towards true meditation is concentration. This first step is comparable on some levels to devotion. The next step from concentration is letting go OF the concentrating itself and the surrender into whatever may be the present moment experience.

So, then we can say that devotion is binary just as concentration is. There is a mind and a candle flame. There is a devotee who is aiming the praise at the statue of God's nature and if you cannot sense the nature there is no purpose. These are binary and based in duality. The Oneness is the closing off of the separation into the ultimate reality that knows nothing but itself, but the grace I suppose is that it is Love for its own sake, I think of the mayan Ouroboros as an image. You could say God Loves God itself. I have always said that Love may be wise for many reasons based in time but in the moment of it, it has no other things going on but itself, being Love and becoming more Love unto itself, which is essentially the desire of every soul, to be wrapped in Love. Love is infectious and we will all be its prey, I suppose.

You may have heard of different paths that people have chosen throughout ancient time and in the here and now. I feel grace when I am in the presence of devotion and it is one of the most luscious choices because it is akin to a flower, the flower being your soul and heart chakra, blooming and revealing a gorgeous fragrance that grows as your allusions about God pass away. Another reason this topic is so exciting for me in this very book is because it is common throughout all lands and beliefs.

We see God projected into our dimension as a Hanuman or a Jesus Christ or a * Green Tara Avalokiteshvara but that is essentially the redemptive Love of God like the * Sistine Chapel by Michelangelo in which God extends his perfectly merciful hand out to all of humankind represented by the man perceiving God from heaven as separate. Even though we may be perceiving through our senses which are bound to our bodies in this Earth plane we actually begin to strengthen our divine mind perception when we move with all our desire toward God. And God knows we are involved in that and sometimes either obviously or subtly extends a hand out to our heart.

Something that comes to me is the perspective of God loving us the way we are meant to love everyone else. What I mean is that if God loves us in a certain and unique way; what we can call is subjective and that way will be a guideline for how we are to love the world in general. Quite an interesting concept. This is interesting to consider and would be great but something about it is curious…so if we consider the inverse, if God loved us all purely objectively –

I had a conversation with a friend today, a great friend that is a blessing to all, I mentioned the love of God and expressed my mind on it. "What if God loved everyone the same way, like if God was a vending machine you go up to and put your thumb on it and out pops your packet of divine love…" The point I was trying to make with this was -that might not be so grand (to say the least). So, then what are our options here, God loves us so perfectly that it is not a burden on us or on God either. As any relationship is designed for, its purpose is to be a win-win, the intimacy is the ticket to ride and the relationship and is both the ocean and the ship on which we are traveling to the destination of God. The point of all of these relationships as I said earlier in this book in the passage titled "relationships" I mentioned in the beginning that all relationships are divine because it all leads to God, ultimately.

Devotion is the pinnacle of this when someone no longer has another human companion to be with. To give oneself to God in song, in the rosary, in the yoga, in the tai chi, in whatever perfect passion you have that God is well aware of is the path your heart has decided upon to finally embrace

God as yourself. Essentially your higher self is a higher vibrational perspective that can be as a bridge into the vastness of the reality of empty awareness and the heart of God and, by the way, this is proper preparation for our body's death on a spiritual level. This is like looking at the directions before you go on a trip.

Why is being devoted better, perhaps, then remaining neutral to God? You may have heard idle hands are the devils playgrounds. The Truth in this sentiment is that if someone has too much freedom without a setting of goals they will end up falling into mis-qualifications of energetic expression. For example, if a young boy sits at home alone and has nothing to foster his growth he will most likely and naturally so create difficulty for himself or others, but the reason this is happening is not because he is a "bad" boy, the reason this is happening is because the community is failing him. It is more important to teach a child to be kind than to 'win' at every game. (Don't get me wrong, I am ultra-competitive as well) They will become naturally defensive, territorial, and unwelcoming because they will see everyone as a threat they must defeat to win the "love" of their parental figure.

I will ask you this - is it more important to learn to accept defeat or to win? I believe that the first is more crucial because you will not emotionally have the intelligence to succeed if you never face surrender head on and with full awareness and love and joy, be defeated to win the humble victory with God. Jesus lost his body, Buddha lost his mind.

You may be "the best" but you will not be the happiest! This is because real joy has absolutely no dependence on if you win or lose. For example, if you win, be happy, if you lose, be happy. Both are reasonable and possible. Once we realize that community is the great success, to foster growth for all beings. The games we play are for fun and should be taken only as seriously as the growth of that soul demands within the safety of that community. This is like when the samurai students practice sparring with sticks.

Returning this into a perspective relevant to devotion and the question I posed "Why is being devoted better, perhaps, then remaining neutral to God?" The answer is because being devoted to God will actually benefit you more. God is a real and conscious being that sometimes demands our recognition and respect, why would you, already knowing of God, ignore that? Unless you are still feeling hurt and you blame God (which makes sense)? I often say that God, of all beings, can take your pain, your judgment, your hatred, and turn it into surrender and wash you every morning in prayer and in reverence and in songs. You can actually learn to have healthy human (and animal) relationships based off of your pure and perfectly honest relationship with God! If that isn't something for everyone in society and community I don't know what is… thank you for considering my heart of devotion- which is where the wisdom comes out of.

35
ADVAITA VEDANTA/NON-DUAL SPIRITUAL TEACHINGS AND TEACHERS

I learned through google search just now that Advaita Vedanta is a branch of Hinduism. But do not get religiously dismayed by this because it has much more profound implications and scope than any one belief system or school of thought. And if it helps you the teachers never once seemed to mention that it stems from Hinduism so it must not be too important to the overall message of this particular philosophy.

I have studied many teachings from a handful of spiritual teachers who resonate with this way of living life and relating to existence. It seems to be very simple, which is relaxing and helpful because people don't need more confusion they DO need liberation though. Vedanta seems to be based in a reduction of the mind into its most basic way of seeing and eventually its relation to what is sees as separate and then the removal of the illusion of the separate state as a dream and the remaining Truth of Oneness as the reality that lasts; that is real. I guess the only value that can be derived from this way of relating to everything is if it makes you more joyful and more kind ... to yourself, which ends up being everything, haha. You ARE everything else. I must say the relief that can flow from this perspective is VERY important because it is not conducive for judgment at all. If we are all One who are we judging? And why?

You see that there will always, for some time, be another experience to have, another book to read, another sentence to think up, and another dimension to explore, but when that fades away the simplicity is very obvious and aware of itself, that is the message of Advaita vedanta. It can be shocking to a lot of people because the judging mind doesn't have a leg to stand on. You will end up realizing something that might be difficult to accept if you steep in this perspective for sometime but maybe that which you were afraid of losing wasn't for your greater benefit. I enjoy * Mooji, Adyashanti, Francis Bennet, Papaji, and Gangaji. They are my experience of Vedanta. The reason I believe this way of teaching is popular is because it is what we can ALL relate to, rather than a handful.

We are all conscious. The other day I had an insightful and necessary conversation with a school friend, we crossed paths for a specific reason, it seems the Universe needed something from me. I ended up walking his mind into the perspective of Non-dual teachings in which the point is to see clearly the awareness of the Self and to not get distracted by the content of that seeing. For example, the point I seemed to be giving to him on this bus ride was the lack of requirements that sincere joy has.

> "You can sit in that space of pure consciousness and feel inherently joyful without any external cause." – It is a possible thing.

This is something that is a common message of these teachers, the reason this message seems to remain the same throughout the ageless time is because Truth is beyond space and time, the guru's name and face change but the Truth they aim to convey is the same for everyone.

The food you eat may be a different dish but it is still caloric intake, does this make sense? It seems that these teachers have to have a lot of personality because they say a lot for not having really much to say. For example, they are almost like the people that are entertaining the souls in the waiting room before entering into heaven, which I mean to be the pure consciousness bliss, also known as Satchitananda. *

A highly recommended video to enjoy is the divine laughter videos available on youtube. The videos document the apparent removal of the ego in which the heart seems to find this very funny and the laughter sometimes goes on for many minutes.

There is something called Satsang that is a period of time designated for the removal of the ego but I suppose it is really a connection with Truth that is deeper than our personal problems and separation. This is important because we all could use a distinct meeting for this exact and divine purpose in which we not only can have our problems "solved" but better yet we can see that they aren't a big deal much at all in a bigger vision of Reality... no offense "problems". The word Satsang translates as "communion with Truth" -this is the name still used by the sages and wise people even today. I have a video of my own (Dr. Joe Vertino) LOG OF MEDIA*

I guess even simpler would be the silent time. The two most influential "silent" gurus I can think of were * Neem Karoli Baba and Sri Ramana Maharshi.

Both of them did not fancy speaking but they were very influential, nonetheless, why is that? (I say 'is' because their love and wisdom carries on still). I believe that the basic teachings can be like pointers but when one is ready for the real thing the words become sounds, they carry no power and eventually silence is all there is. And in the words of my wise good friend "the things will happen to you until you stop asking 'why'". What this means is that you don't have to make something that is temporary into something more than what it is. And the wisdom of silence is that in its nakedness and purity we are all made more pure and naked in our essence.

One saying is *the reason troubles happen is for one reason, people haven't learned to sit in a room and be happy with nothing." (by Blaise Pascal) The reason for all of the war and all of the division is because people don't yet grasp the quality and nature of reality, meaning the actual as opposed to the ephemeral joys.

This is the joy that comes from nowhere and goes to nowhere. Have you ever seen silence appear or disappear? Have you ever found its source? How can you make a belief system out of silence? Why is that even necessary? And if you are mentally tired then thank God for that. Something that I have been taught and have experienced is the dropping down (of the awareness) from the head to the heart and finally to the Hara where it rests. This is very clearly delineated with *Adyashanti. He is all about that. I remember he spoke about the last step in the ego was like a fist that was clenched and was an energetic "No" And is the last barrier between what we see as "us" and what we see as "God" is this resistance to the absence of resistance; meaning the pure ground of being of consciousness without resistance to any experience. This does not mean that when you finally surrender to the totality of God that you have no more personal traits or hobbies or preferences it means that you no longer separate what YOU prefer from what happens to be the case already, in some ways.

There are many people that "grow up" never learning this ability and grace of dancing with the Lord. Because it really is akin to dancing to the music of Universal Love and soul growth as we make decisions and as we develop independence, autonomy, and individuality within the context of our circumstances.

The last point I would like to make here is - What if you and your situation had no distance between it?

What this means is that you no longer alienate yourself from the present moment. I do guarantee you that it is necessary IF you care about moving through life without nagging thoughts of resentment, anger, jealousy, and general disdain for anybody including your own self. This is essentially what it means to be an adult on this planet. Because only when we are able to be fully present will we be the perfect parents we want to be. The value of this book, which I see as infinite, is also exemplified when relating to children. Have you ever noticed how often your mind made beliefs interfere with you and children, who don't have these same beliefs? The grace in speaking with an open heart to children is that they can reset your mind. They have the ability to create in you a clean heart and to give you your original mind back. The reason this works with Advaita Vedanta is because it takes away the illusory gap of beliefs between you and anything else, especially children. Ram ram.

This is the Ying Yang symbol

36
ATTAINING AND GENERATING BALANCE

Something that is quite a hot topic is seeking, finding, and maintaining balance in all aspects of life and death. I would be overjoyed to bring in the shamanic perspective. They essentially have it rough. They are the Universes punching bags until they transcend properly and then they are unstoppable. Pretty simple. So, the Shamanic path chooses you not the other way around. The reason for this is because ego death is a prerequisite. So, the reason I said life and death earlier is because of this. The people who have the most balance tend to be those who have not as much qualms with existence and the ending of said existence. I have been contemplating the end, and I have to say I seem to be quite happy with it, at any time at all. This is not suicidal, this is realistic, and actually mature.

The point may be extreme but it is useful to you if you want it to be. Balancing the little self with the big Self is crucial for this to make sense. When we are seeking health from yoga but we are spiritually ignoring ourselves we may be doing it wrong as a process of soul liberation. This is what happens when people do yogic asanas but they do not include the Spirit. So, the reason I mention this is because the formless is just as pertinent to attain perfect balance as the form and also complete self -Love. Once again the Love is what calms the mind after it has been heard, The Love is what creates and destroys, including our nirvana and our non-nirvana.

The real answer for this is Zen, if pure Zen happened upon you would you even recognize it? And then would you surrender into it for all eternity meaning- just now? I feel the smirk on my face and I know that there is a divine purpose to every experience and that to stand in the middle of it is a good choice. To be aware of beginnings and endings as the same. The judgement may exist for a little while and then where will you put your thoughts? If you were completely comfortable in anything that would be a taste of Zen living. To be fully serious and to be completely unserious, to be always aware and in Love with the presence whether it matters or not.

The heart chakra is the center point for a reason. It stabilizes all the other ones, the energy vortexes we have known as chakras, which means spinning wheel by the way. I am now sitting in a chapel and there is a pitch black Jesus with his arms wide open and Mother and Father on each side. The usefulness of balance is to move from point A to point B with as little pain as possible and eventually to allow existence to be good enough, meaning we don't have to do anything to it as if we were separate.

The allusion I would like to dispel about balance is the concept and attachment to stillness. If you ever watch someone do tai Chi you can sense that they are still while they are moving their body around. This is the weird factor. Balance does not demand anything, in fact balance is actually constantly being reasserted by existence.

The new age people call this alignment. To have a straight spinal column and to have one vertebrae gently and securely balanced on top of the next is chiropractic alignment. But also, do not fantasize about a future self. To have balance on every level is what I am talking about here.

The question I would like to have answered is why does balance matter? For example, have you looked at your alterior motives for this balance attaining? If it is to be right it is to bring you closer to the divine. If it is because you don't feel acceptable in your group of friends, you may want to consider finding a new more resonant and welcoming group to reside in. I dare say that the acceptance of yourself now is almost more important than the balance itself- even though that can be our highest pursuit- but we are certainly not ever going to be okay by segregating our insides; like causing that worst ailment of <u>thee inauthentic schism</u>.

The paradox; the balance you are seeking and the acceptance of your present state… the latter may be more crucial for both the attainment OF the balanced state and the irrevocable joy that surrounds all souls independent of attainments. I mean what would you expect a laundry list of steps for balance? Step 1. Meditate until you no longer want to get up. 2. Go about your day. This is useful and even though there is sarcasm in this I am not wrong. But in your heart you don't want to be robotic do you? You want freedom. I understand this desire and need to be free.

What if you gave yourself permission to be completely okay with the state of everything, always? The cool thing is we fear we would end up annihilated but we would actually end up being ecstatic if we choose to live this way.* "Animals as Leaders" is one of my favorite bands. And their lead guitarist, Tosin Abasi's favorite band is also mine; Meshuggah. The concept of Animals as Leaders is useful for the purpose of tuning into balance. As the name suggests; The natural state is in equilibrium, and all is well with the world. The Animal Kingdom is a gateway for us to come into balance and harmony. So, why do attuning ourselves to our chosen Animal spirit assist us in this endeavor? It is useful because as I am typing these special words I am slightly or severely channeling. I am channeling the energies of nature, the snake, the Goat, The Lion.

The energy YOU need to find balance. The animal self is not evil or wrong it is honest. If you felt that, you, as a human being, were doing better than all of mother nature you would be mistaken. We must live as One. The reason is on one level I am excited by animals, they are divine and can sense things that are important. But the most important reason is because our self-talk is negative, and animals do not condone that behavior.

The animals are essentially fully themselves, we on the other hand, seem to fluctuate in authenticity from my perspective. But if we are going to live in a proper way we should stop going to extremes and find our own homeostasis. The great impediment of this homeostasis is self judgement. IF we dabbled in self-love we would quickly change our vibrational frequency and we would realize that our judgements are not as necessary as our uniqueness. So, when we allow ourselves the space and freedom to grow we will be in balance. I highly recommend meditating upon one or several specific earth based animals.

I have faith that this will set some things correct within you and that it will become very simple and obvious to you what natural homeostasis feels like AND importantly what taking true help from another source outside of yourself feels like- and it is many times best to start with something kind of dead like an animal who cannot truly "KNOW" YOU. But you still are allowing the reach outside of yourself in TRUST. Psychologists would agree because really this is the preferred "vibration" or pattern of human consciousness and is technically the foundation of ALL TALK THERAPY- yet it is something we are not masters of and are spiritually pulled into it for it is a need.

So, as you come into a streamlined way of following your highest excitement you begin to develop a thrilling sense of freedom, autonomy, and full on relief. You may want to consider the most simple manner of conducting yourself until you have been grounded in the deep peace and perfection of reality; which is the primary aspect of Balance. What I mean by this is that adding things onto your day may not be nearly as smart as taking some things away - if you feel off balance that is. God gives and God taketh away. Om namo Shivaya aum. Then as you may have attuned or studied the animal kingdom with simply only yourself and sincerity in heart- you can even branch out to God and still remain even deeper (eventually) connected to an animal or animals! God is, and perhaps just knowing that is surely enough (for this lifetime).

"There are many great people throughout beautiful history we have known that are shining examples of balance and are great to us all because of this reason alone- Giving Joy to the world like the great Christmas song- It is almost New Years now when I am finishing this book. The tumult of Life is something that we must do something about - always! This is what Buddha called mara- the root of unnecessary suffering(s). There is nothing we can do about the winds and the waves but the disruptions between us and our pure observation of them – is tumult and must be gently and powerfully worked away on all levels!

The only way it goes away is if we do something about it but also if we do not in the sense that more of you it takes without perhaps eventually concern for yourself. And one day you may wake up and completely forget about everything else and a smile with some perhaps sadness and creeping away goes your heart to the floor… The resonance this is profound for it can be the most real you have ever felt.

"The reality it feels Good." Says that one person alone. Forever alone no one ever there forever. Jai- Victory.

The authenticity of you can rise right away and manage everything!

The righteousness of God is found in that great choice to be pleased by the right things in your life. Balance comes in this way alone- for it is honorable and makes you want to be seen and heard be enjoyed by the sunshine and the people. Then it is the same energy and way in the Tai Chi Qi Gong master and he must be seen for you to learn it from him or her from age to age to go out his own house!

Then you having it in your own journey is like a symbol of purity and reliability even though you are not the master and all of his/her choices.

The complexities whether they are dealt with or not (properly yet) of any possible world you can lay them down there and see just how you are in tai chi qi gong- the greatness of the Universe is not your business to make happen for it is there Do not waste an eye movement towards the heavens.

But… rather realize your own incompletion and seek no further than the trustworthy and trusting figure the MASTER in front of you.

Then practice in a great tradition and make sure it is before you become devoted and sincerely speak its name in the streets- but know this the only reason you could ever need is the name of this chapter ; Simply ATTAINING AND GENERATING BALANCE.

If you have faith and listen but you will be making your own first perhaps and not only wise choice in all your life. The sincerity and the awakenings and the embellishment of your soul that God will perfectly lay on your tree your branch your limb alone forever to make heaven that is perfect be realized on this here planet, thee Earth! It is the same Universal Truth foundational for all of the major traditions that pertain to eventual enlightenment right and proper - thus!

ArchAngel Michael is the leader just as the master is in charge and we have to look at them - and Trust, amen. Long live the divine relationships from age to age of authentic mentorship, with great respect and love- my favorite prayer, amen.

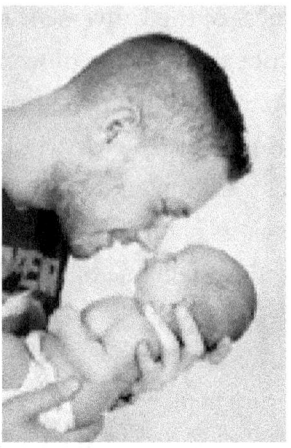

What a lovely position for a parent to be in towards their child- a BOW.

37
PARENTING AND FAMILY RELATIONS

This is eternally relevant. We all have experienced childhood, and the process known as individuation, and we are biologically responsible to procreate and raise children; also known as parenting (though we are currently overpopulated). All of this takes place within a family structure. And we should have no doubts, fears, guilt, and/or shame in any way about this eternally relevant process and all of its intricacies. I mention in the last excerpt that to be a good parent requires full focused attention on the present moment.

Even if you do not consider yourself spiritual and believe that "love" is a chemical reaction within the brain you still cannot deny the fact that if your mind, feelings, beliefs, and thought structure is taking you elsewhere while your child is in front of you that is not helpful to the safety and overall well-being of your family structure. There is a time for day dreaming and it is not when your child is exploring a playground. The only obvious reason your mind may wander in boredom is because you may have a perpetuating useless belief that "you" as an adult are "so beyond" this simple playground.

But I challenge you to consider playing again with your child, I wholeheartedly believe that if you genuinely had fun you would be ensuring the safety and fostering the growth of that child. Because when you are involved with the child you should be fully involved.

As much as I love my family, and my parents who did an actually great job raising me I have some somewhat traumatic experiences that were instilled in my memory involving my parents. They did not wish to harm my psyche but I would say the apparent lack of awareness and fulfillment in the present moment allowed them to hurt some feelings of mine from time to time.

The most obvious one was in response to my carefree self and when I wanted to be open and care-free and jokingly saying things out my window to a woman passerby I remember saying that the Bills are gonna win the football game and I shouted out the window to her "Spread it!" And my Dad immediately scorned me very aggressively and I shut up. I don't think that was necessary, Dad. I feel that if he was upset at me he could have made a small remark and then later on, discussed it with me face to face not during the car ride there.

I don't have any recollection if we had won or lost but the memory remains. So, if we are being simply honest we can see that cycles of abuse are our choice to continue or to heal with our free will and present moment awareness. God loves us and as I said earlier this love is what can release the bonds we may have been feeling on an instinctual level that lead to pain continuing.

I pray we can somehow find a true sense of safety among all these varying experiences and can make decisions for ourselves that come from our heart. This is a good segue for me to discuss individuation.

Individuation is the process by which children become individuals and learn to set themselves apart from their parents, especially, and other children around them also. Only when someone has been fully individuated can they make actual wholehearted decisions and these decisions will be in alignment with Love first and foremost because they are no longer swayed by peer pressures or societal/family agendas.

They have the present moment and that is all they need to make a clear and successful choice and they can live happily in that freedom and this can foster some real family experiences that assist this Earth to grow properly by outlining healthy family relationships. This may be the most crucial aspect of individuation because it fosters independence without spite and a self-chosen autonomy. To move beyond people, places, and things and to stand in your own feet is to be an individual. To look at the world with only YOUR eyes, is to be an individual. To move beyond the distracting and unnecessary thought patterns of self-doubt, is individuality. So, when someone is an individual they are more safe because they are not as easily if at all swayed against their own principles and values, which tend to be wholesome and caring and not overly selfish as some would project. The reason for this is because most people will do harm when struggling to be free, unknowingly scratching others as they struggle to be free from society's restraints.

The great man,* Tomas Haake, the drummer and lyricist of Meshuggah exemplifies this perfectly. He says in his album Catch Thirty Three "The struggle to free myself from restraints becomes my very shackles". This is a very mature spiritual mindset; it means that you accepting your present state is what will end the torture, the Chinese fingertrap will be powerless over your fingers when they stop resisting. And then you move inward, like the Buddha says "Inquire within". You begin the healing process, which is only accessible when it is done with your free will between God and yourself, mostly. I say mostly because therapy and energy workers can activate certain energies that are conducive for the healing process and the enlightened mind journey back to completion.

And your family and all families are made up of these individuals.
*Confucius says "There will be Peace in the world when there is peace in

the nations, there will be peace in the nations when there is peace in the communities, there will be peace in the communities when there is peace in the families, and there will be peace in the family when there is peace in the heart." So, my aim is peace of heart, peace of soul, peace of mind; Buddha mind. To love oneself is to love the self in another as well. Zen lifestyle.

Even if we are the enlightened black sheep of our family structure we still are asked to return for thanksgiving or Christmas, or perhaps we still live near or even with our immediate family still. The socio-dynamics of family is potentially very sensitive because there is a dependency on many levels until we grow out of that efficiently. Choices that we make are reflections of our level of consciousness. This helps foster compassion when we see ourselves or others this way. I sometimes explain Christ as a level of self-awareness that Jesus, Buddha, Melchizedek, and many others throughout endless time have touched or resided in. This Christ consciousness is delineated by *Drunvalo Melchizedek in the different levels of consciousness in which he uses sacred geometry to portray, also known as "squaring the circle" which can be understood in his book "The Ancient Secret of the Flower of Life". So, if we can be in our larger divine mind when we are physically and emotionally involved with family we will be operating from a higher mind that has a higher goal and scope at large. This is beneficial for many reasons and will lessen the potential harm and will take advantage of opportunities for growth.

*I know Eckhart Tolle takes on the pain body and during interviews and responds to people's questions using the wisdom of the power of now. He says when the pain body becomes inflamed the tranquil presence can be turned up and this will hopefully soothe the aches and pains that may or may not be generational or even ancestral in nature. This is a situational remedy or defense from the downward pulling force of our ego mind when it is agitated, instead of shaming this we should open our heart of compassion and be still and listen. The actual process for healing these ancestral wounds can be healed with a good Reiki healer.

The great nature of the Reiki energy and white light is that it goes where it is needed, no questions asked, and the Reiki healer does not have to "aim" the energy, it goes where it goes. And since you have, like a computer, a memory bank in which your DNA has some potential harmful patterns stored- Reiki can and will eventually heal those. You just have to be lucky enough and willing enough to be healed in this way for the greater good of the Earth.

The divine masculine and divine feminine are relevant here; they are the archetypes of the man and woman who have come into their power and have essentially stepped up to the cosmic plate. The people that have chosen or are chosen to embody this essence are way showers because they are examples of how to love, serve, and protect everybody properly as any righteous mother or father does. A divine masculine man will naturally stand in between harm and any child, he will be strong and proud. A divine feminine woman will be open and gentle to any child and will defend them with her life and heart. The goal is for beings to encapsulate BOTH of these.

This is simple to perceive but takes a lifetime of dedication to pursue and accomplish, but I hope it happens for you now! Some spiritual gurus like Zen master Rama, also known as *Dr. Frederick Lenz, had given some insight on this topic. It can be found through his zen tapes collection from the 80's. In it he discusses the last step of enlightenment, the merging of the two sides,

I remember something like the thought of the seemingly overly masculine Tibetans of old and how the more they came toward God and nirvana they became more feminine and gentle and pleasant rather than stiff and rigid. The reason this applies to this entry is because we all possess these points of balance. And as I said in an earlier section, balance is always occurring, just as healing is always occuring. The reason meditation "heals" is because healing is a natural and constant part of reality, in meditation we are just getting into the flow of that process with all our mind and will. Do you ever look at someone while they are meditating and wonder what they are doing? They are willing the healing to occur, which it is. Balance comes from the inside out, when you transform yourself you give all others the opportunity to do the same, especially your family who believe they "know" the real you. Perhaps, perhaps not.

> The Buddha returned to his father after his journey was completed and he fully transcended and his father looked at him and he looked at his father, and he said that the Buddha had changed, and he agreed and said the entire (level of) consciousness has changed. And I would like to add the only thing that doesn't change is Love. That is its Power - you can always count on it. And that is the REAL you. Ram ram.

"You may have noticed that the focus of this chapter has been; individual nature- why is that Dr. Joe? Why not a psychological portrayal of family dynamics? Because the great wisdom of the ages arises in all single people by that way alone and parenting is nothing without it- the family relationships are something we should and innately wish to carry on through our individual lives. Some new age people would say that is our "pre-birth" intention! Thee agenda of God is to prosper just like any sincere family. And knowing our self deeper and deeper ALWAYS 100% fosters that! The soothing nature of good family relationships and the great balm of a man or woman who has known that for years is so pleasant to everyone outside of the family.

This world is like that playground and you dear parent deserve to be moving in parallel with other beings like a Gazelle running across its natural habitat- and when your running is done then you having restful awareness are in a passive place to receive your children and prosper in speech and wisdom adopt give up on your own alone. I am so proud of myself and the way that I love the reader; a parent who is in need of my help. The way it helps is by enlivening yourself - the great despair of all parenting is its opposite the deadening and lack of ability to share and a perhaps isolating feeling inside - we could say for many reasons for life has many but we know it isn't the fault of our children alone for they simply just came into the world but don't give up on the way of education and itself my main message; HOPE!

The relief of knowing it is never ever your journey; your children's!

That there is really no guilt in that for it is simply God's will and we can't be educated otherwise. And we are not "meant to" but simply ARE in newness- everyday!

And some homework or assignment is to give in to that newness with all of your aspects, which includes your parenting! And you will come to eventually find differences, holes in the continuum of bullshit, which is mind conditioning that attacks the authentic and lives only by way of perpetuated lying beliefs!

How exciting to read that: So, the first and only step truly is being willing to be in total control as you are now a parent FOREVER! And to snap out of the lie that you are pre-made like some frozen product but you are much better off being so anxiety ridden and in alignment :) with the divine will which is a constant path for ALL SOULS to be liberated!

The true move the only one is thus; not be afraid of your own positive changes when you now have your children! And to say guide clearly; that means to be willing to be inclusive of other parents and see the world as not a threat especially to your children but to grab at the world so as to obtain for the benefit of your children! And you can see how all of this is oscillating around the individual nature, inevitably.

Drunvalo Melchizedek- Strong Positive influence (who was very emotional on camera from time to time- it was awesome)

38
THE IMPORTANCE OF SELF-EXPRESSION

Today in therapy I participated in a group that decided to emotionally go off the rails. My friend was defending his choice of a role model and the group decided to be hateful rather than helpful... even though the most difficult moments can be what tests our true meddle. I ended up becoming upset also but for a different reason, I did not feel like allowing people's unconsciousness to cause pain and so I chose for sometime to fight, and eventually I decided to meditate. But, I've noticed through my years of blossoming that groups will do something very distracting when they sense strong Truth in one person.

The Truth in that individual will end up healing the ego resistance of the entire room, but today in my group I decided to defend what I saw as my friend being severely judged. I feel that people are in desperate need of healing and that sometimes it comes to a particular point in which they have to stop hurting other people and realize that healing is no longer a request it is what we need to focus on to move forward as a species, as individual points of God, as a collective, and as souls who incarnated on Earth for at least one lifetime and also because we deserve it. We deserve to be whole and to wake up- or vice versa if you meditate in the mornings- Haha.

I feel that sometimes "Light-workers*" decide to sit peacefully rather than get their minds involved in the work of defending the pure light of awareness.

In today's group I did both when called upon by the divine wisdom within me and all of the pain reflected around me. I spoke up and also quieted down. Both seemed right at the time and you can see that the Love is primary in this experience because when people don't feel safe they can go to extremes. When I intend to make people safe I use all of my heart. This doesn't seem to fail. I believe that the topic I have chosen for this is special; self-expression is essential for energetic equilibrium. I am a person who likes to use simple and reliable logic. I weigh the pros and the cons of holding in my feeling or releasing it into the space around me. I feel that the perspective of love is what I am inherently, and I feel that provides safety, abundance and a divine purpose that I am willing to share with everyone.

I believe that God as the creator is blessing me in every moment now more than ever, because I feel that God is my focal point. And when I look into myself I find God. And when I express myself I express an aspect of God. When I show love I allow myself to become one with God. This is the importance of self-expression when it is aligned properly with God's will which seems to be love and mercy itself.

A lot of my intention for my own self-expression, which is all the words I write for you, is to bring about the shift and energy necessary to remove the blockages of other people's self-expression. So, if I am doing my job right you should feel an energy change perhaps in your heart or anywhere, doesn't matter where, and then you may want to discuss something personal or heartfelt with a loved one or friend. This would be lovely.

I feel that to use our free will to create consciously a more beautiful existence is a very real and relevant form of love. The world seeks peace, harmony, and balance, but first we need to find a sense of self that is healthy.

What I mean by this is that we have a sense of self that may be very rude, upset, naive, or overly judgmental but this can be transmuted and aligned in a way to a more conducive sense of self that is seeking Truth, purity, honesty, and overflowing joy and abundance. This is part of my mission on Earth. You may call me a "starseed*" or whatever you want but that is why I exist. I am the love of God in the form of a human being who is incarnated and has collected many experiences within my soul's heart to share with you. I am willing to be open and vulnerable for the sake of love as it is. I have no desire to be ashamed. I have no desire to demand anything from existence. I am simply here enjoying my life and I love to write, to play, to teach and to learn.

That is who I am. Who are you? Do you know that I love you? I am in love with existence completely! I often dish out spiritual exercises; one that is great is seeing God in others… The tricky part is focusing on that and then watching as the upsetting words come out of their mouth, haha. You might not want to hear about their political stance but you are seeing deeper than that, beyond that into them, the reality of GOD.

I am sure you have heard of the psychological phenomena of the bystander effect and/or the girl who cried wolf. These are interesting in relation to self- expression. There once was a woman who was being assaulted outside of a big apartment building full of people, she screamed for help and many neighbors heard her but they did not call the police because they believed someone else, someone different would alert the authorities. The woman ended up in a bad way because in all seriousness no-one called the police in this specific case. How strange and sad. The next example is the girl who cried wolf, when there is someone who continues to abuse their God given power of self-expression they are doing a disservice to the community. When the girl cries out a warning and people respond but it is not a real warning and she does this several times… she loses her credit with the people of that community and the risk is that her word is tarnished. Her honor may be damaged for some time.

And more seriously she cannot be so effective in giving out real warnings in the future. These two are examples of psychological phenomena that exist that relate to everyone who is capable of self-expression. The first has to do with response to another and the second has to do with your own self-expression. If we choose to move too far into our idea of what we expect other people to be doing in response - we end up becoming guilty of the bystander effect. And conversely if we become too concerned with our freedom of expression at the risk of the community we end up risking the safety and honor in our word as with the girl who cried wolf for example.

These are guidelines, or bumpers for our consciousness to respect and learn from.

The goal is not always perfection. Sometimes the goal is honor. Sometimes the goal is dignity and respect, understanding. And this is what the moment calls for. And more importantly you will notice the energy in you moving through you will be a clue as to what is right. This is the wisdom of following your own excitement. It provides you with a sense of integrity and autonomy and a joyous freedom that we can share with children and teach them the rules of our universe, that are meant to support us if we will respect and apply them efficiently. But once again, we see the big picture, and from God's heart-mind we can perceive with less concerns, and proceed with alert attention for no other reason but our own inherent joy.

The rules are necessary for the expansion of yourself and everyone as well. When they stop serving that purpose they are no longer rules they are ego enforced restrictions that any truly honorable person would willingly break, on purpose. There is an inherent order to existence and it is not found squarely in our current government system. You becoming an individual is the first step. Then you maturing is the next step.

Then you becoming gentle and compassionate is the lasting step. And eventually you will realize greater and greater levels of wisdom and divine Truth and have the courage of soul to share them with others around you or even write it all down! This process eliminates the abuse of power we have put up with on Earth.

As I mentioned earlier in this book, in the section called "The Power of Being Weird" (Page 33) I said under the cons of being weird consciously is that one must surrender their fear of the unknown. And quite simply seen- the unknown is something we are almost always in contact with, so why should we fear that?

A lot of these ideas that we have pertaining to government are an excuse for individuals who never quite allowed their soul to be fully engulfed in new and unknown experiences. You can see from those who are enthralled by real adventures that they lack this stress and desire to control circumstances that are none of their business to attempt to control at all. So, moving forward within this context we can use our power of aware choice properly and decide with all of our awareness and being… what house to buy, what dish to order, what show to watch, what book to read, what person to talk to, and on and on.

And then we can choose when our time for rest is upon us to allow the rest to be fully enjoyed, without fear, guilt, and shame. We become participants in existence rather than victims - then we are truly adults, on a global and cosmic scale.

Someone like Buddha or Jesus is deserving of some attention in this section because they are people that spoke and used their power of voice and self-expression in a big way. And if we would all feel so comfortable and strong we could all do that and then we wouldn't feel as needing to judge them for trying to desperately help us as a planet. I feel when self-expression becomes unleashed we will release all of our negative tendencies eventually all that will come to the light in some loving way.

We can resonate with energy that we ourselves enjoy and choose to surround yourself with so that is my goal, one of them, is to allow people to feel so comfortable that we can be ourselves fully and see how special we all are, both as individuals and as a great collective body. Self-expression is a crucial process that we can work with to seek out and locate our heart and in this we find our perfected balance. And at the end of the day do you really prefer a world of people who are hiding their light and genuine love? My answer is a stiff no.

39
THE IMPORTANCE OF BEAUTY

This is a thrilling subject. I have found this to be severely important, more important than it seems. You would think beauty is just some kind of take it or leave it phenomena but in reality it is closer to the Truth than most science is. Unless the science is just so beautiful then the point is moot.

Beauty is the most sophisticated form of unconditional love. It has the power to create mountains, in paintings. It has the ability to immediately stop suffering when God uses it for that. It has the ability to take us beyond words and into the formless in which there is a sense of serenity, and may I remind you here (to invite you deeper into your own heart) all the beauty in the world is an aspect and reflection of you! I know this. So, I thought I would take this topic for a spin in a different, more impactful light. Instead of ranting and raving about all the art in existence I thought I would share my personal opinion as it unfolds within these words, in the here and now. I believe that Art is not synonymous with beauty, but they have crossovers, like parallel dimensions.

I see Art as a general scope that is more of a canvas and less of a point in itself. It is like the blank pages of this book that these words are written on. Beauty is born into our world through art. The beauty itself is a harmonization or the juicy center that comes eventually from the intention or choice to produce something artistic. And I mean ALL art here, not just painting... music, sculpture, film etc. I feel that God uses beauty to bring us into alignment again because when we are young we see most things as beautiful and why did that stop? Because our priorities and our sense of what is really important got tainted, more or less. The journey into enlightenment is actually a returning to our child nature. You should see the yogi gurus in India that laugh and when they laugh they are children, forever. I believe that with all my heart.

I gave a reason why beauty is important to us because we are immediately brought back to source, we fall in love with everything again and we actually begin to be used by creation or you could say used by beauty to create more of itself everywhere we walk. This is the same as when you use a candle flame to light others, it does not diminish. I believe that the joy inherent in all reality is synonymous with this concept. So, you could see this as a cop out, that I am just mashing all these topics together and coming to the same point, which isn't wrong, but that wouldn't be enough of a motivation for me to continue writing, would it? I feel that I am writing all these words because it is not me trying to achieve something but rather it is the natural consequence of me fully tuning into myself as Love. Love wishing the good of the other, being you.

I am writing these words because they are beautiful and they are wise, I am writing these words because they are important and necessary. I am writing for you and for me and for bliss and ecstasy. I am writing because I am in bliss and I can't help but share that. And as you fall in love with the presence of God you find beauty in everything, even pain! I feel the longing to be with the beloved as so perfect it is greater than the person experiencing it, in some ways. The love between the lovers is eternal, but they will pass away unless they see into themselves and see they are, in all honesty, Love, itself and Love never dies. The idea of authenticity is linked to beauty.

True beauty is always in alignment with Truth, because is someone beautiful when they are lying to you? No, it seems to be untrue. But when they finally drop all defenses and surrender their lies beauty becomes very present. So, why does beauty matter philosophically rather than just aesthetically? This is the reason; it is used for both enjoyment and enlightenment. A lot of the time we see the journey toward God as ALL experiences, not just the enjoyable ones, which is true. But the mercy of beauty is that it is impossible to miss, beauty is not about anything beside itself, it is pure. And isn't that what spirit is also? Isn't that what God is, what Love is?

> Also beauty on a deeper and more sincere level is what is responsible for all relationships.

Attraction is the basis for them all. We feel a desire to spend time with someone because we feel their vibration and they feel ours, the beauty of existence represented and being desired, hopefully, mutually, by both beings. I believe that it is almost difficult to come up with more words on beauty because it is so simple and so profound and it is complete in itself, so it does not need more words to make it complete, but it needs more words only for the awareness surrounding it to become more aware of itself as beauty.

The funny thing about beauty is that it is a great form of self-love. Have you sat or lied down and put hands on your chest and said "I love you"?. It is great fun. And you can see that if all is One that beauty is what happens when someone, meaning God in human form, really loves itself. There is a very special vibration in these words.

So, when we sit in silence we can see that beauty is not just visual, it is experiential... and maybe transcendent, it is not just a common goal. What beauty is beyond the laws of cause and effect from a meditative perspective, which you are also, so you are beauty also. For example, if I go into deep meditation and sit there, and when I come up into my head and say to my friends with open eyes "I've had a beautiful meditation" that experience is not some drug trip, it is a still silent beautiful joy. This is the vibration I receive from * Paramhansa Yoganandaji; one of my gurus.

He showed me in his words, his eyes and face, in his body language, and in his soul's calling and guiding a still joy that is ever-present and is the essence of beauty in some ways. You could say that, if all we are doing in meditation is "being" and that is "beautiful" then you could say that beauty is "being" itself at its very simplest core and root. The other trick with beauty is that it is subjective also, it is so personal and it is so unknowable too. What I see as beauty may be only for me to see sometimes and other times we have things we all agree upon and collectively label as beautiful.

But the most profound statement about beauty is that it is not trying to improve, alter, or change one particle of the object it is revering as beautiful. This is seeing with the eyes of pure love and devotion and we can see God with these eyes. God bless you, forever.

40
GOVERNMENT

I believe that the philosopher who came up with the idea of * "the philosopher kings" was in the right- his name was Plato. This perspective states that those who are well informed, are well educated, but most of all bright minded should be in the position of rulership if there even should be such a position at all is another question. I believe that the way a lot of this, our Earth government has got off track, is because we have incorrect motivational factors. I never quite understood why all of this was so stressful! If we are doing things to make the world function, or humbly said, to make humanity function, why are we under so much pressure? For example, my job is not any less important than the job of a congressman or woman, but they seem to suffer from stress more, unfortunately, why is that?

I believe we have misplaced "power" (in this case I used quotations because the real power is something that does not come out of distress or cause more of it, by the way). "Chapter 9: Power" in this book is great found on page 24! We have said to our government "here, we don't know what we really want" And in that way we have people that want to be in the limelight, and who want to be in the front row so to speak of the ship that seems to be involved in governing us.

And we see that this experience of Earth is such a one that we cannot so easily say it was this person or this group at this specific time that is the cause of all of this… It is a link of events that you can see chronologically if you prefer. It does not have to be seen that way, you could see it energetically rather. How much of this government was in alignment with expansion, proper laws of creation and destruction and divine timing and how much of it was based in a childish grab for power and control? Do we really need to say more on this?

You can see that I have no intention but the enlightenment of a planet and if the government is something that must be addressed and dealt with then I will do so, with great verve and honor. For example, just because I care a lot about God does not mean I don't care about things like the government. I feel that if it is important to you, meaning anything you find worthy of consistent attention, then I would like to know why, so that I may understand you!

In a very general sense I feel that the realm of politics is so very malleable that it is difficult to find a grounding in anything real. This is the main turn off for me. I feel that when there is a lack of space and tranquility and ease then you have some major problems. I believe that God does not want us to work and suffer and die. I feel that God designed the universe and our souls for expansion and growth, which is one general point of all experiences. I believe that the job you do should match who you are inside and out.

And I am more concerned for the welfare of the minds and hearts of the people than putting in my vote. I am more interested in getting to know the individuals that make up our republic than supporting any unkind speech. I am interested in claiming our sovereign right as beings of the ultimate reality of cosmic awareness and Love to now begin choosing the energy output they prefer to abide in. For example, no one has the power or ability to take away someone's joy or their excitement and there are laws set up, cosmic laws, that we should invest in and maybe we will see that these laws are more than enough for the success of our planetary body called Earth to survive and thrive with great/supreme joys.

I often, recently, have played a mind game with myself called "what would I do if I were in charge?" I believe if ever I get to teach in a school setting I would love to use this as a mind engagement activity quite regularly. I see that a lot of people have this strange idea that somehow they are either not worthy of ruling/being in charge/being the King or Queen or they feel it would be not as fun if they were. I feel that is not quite the case with me and I will tell you why. I am a Leo, I am the Lion hearted King of my domain, and I love God, so everywhere is God and I am in love with

God everywhere and always, why should I be afraid to be seen for who I am?

I believe that this is one of the great challenges any leader will face; being fully vulnerable. Being willing to bare the speech of everyone and doing so with an open heart, a clear mind, and open hands that are gentle and strong.

In Politics we are really looking for safety aren't we? We want to feel we are in good hands don't we? We want to know everything will be alright, right Mom? Right Dad? Yes, my lovely one. We want to be held and comforted, not stressed out and preoccupied. So, how do we trust this? We would need to look at things a bit differently. And recognize the things on a more subtle level rather than waiting until there are mass shootings and wars occurring. For example, if we sense someone is struggling and they are part of our community it is our duty and should be our innate joy to surround them with our loving awareness. Do you really feel that if we did this there would be wars? Why would there be?

> The war in our psyche creates war on our Earth. When we have the guts to stand up to the bully mentality we move beyond it and we reawaken a divine consciousness that is more real than the suits on all the backs of the politicians around the world.

This way of existing from the heart, as the heart is not a political stance, it is the only stance we have left because it is reality and we have been in some illusion for some time.

We must come together as One people and see that there is a time for sparring and debating and it is to expand and to grow our bodies, our souls, and our minds to reach nirvana, it is not something we should make into our entertainment...

People talking on the television and disagreeing constantly is not necessary as we seem to think it is. I wonder how much of this is done for the right reason? To me I seem to keep things simple in my mind, are we being pushed and pulled by love or are we reacting from fear? We, regardless, of our personal differences can at least be willing to agree on this, to see this clearly, to perceive yourself clearly. This should be the true test for any and all people in potential positions of leadership… be very clear on why you have chosen this path for yourself. So, going back to my original words on government, the philosophers should rule. And what is a philosopher, well the word "philosophy" means the study or the love of Truth. So, that should clear things up. People who are motivated by their passion for seeking finding and promoting the TRUTH.

This is where I plant my feet in government and in really all matters. I do not put on one face for politics and another face for my family or friends or students for that matter. I am eternally present and I am here to help in however way I can. I wish all beings to be and feel safe and comforted. I wish that the great love and wisdom of community extends its loving and secure branches to all branches of all governments everywhere and that does instill healing in that love and acceptance.

I also mentioned earlier the laws of the universe of creation and destruction. In one way both creation and destruction are unreal, that both exist within the heart, mind, and will of God as the ultimate reality. But, from our viewpoint we see that things come into existence and they go out of existence, government systems are part of this. So, if something is no longer serving the growth and expansion of the divine will I pray it will be gently and thoroughly destroyed and that would be the most merciful way for humanity to heal fully.

And then in our new hope we may find a sustainable and honest way of relating with each other where all the needs are met sufficiently and where we all can prosper. I pray this new way of living may be set into motion within our cosmic and divine alignment. So, if you truly feel excited to turn on the news, do so! If you truly feel drawn to politics, go for it! There is nothing wrong with that energy of passion! We need you to help us create a more peaceful Earth! Thank you to all the people who have in the past invested their time and energy in government affairs and a blessing on all the children who will be in that realm for our future together! Ram ram.

Dr. Mikao Usui- founder of the Reiki tradition !

41
REIKI HEALING

The main message of this is that Reiki is such a great thing for everyone in the world in every possible way it doesn't require you to know anything more or less, it doesn't require you to feel or be or act differently than you are have been or plan to be! It doesn't require you to "act in its best interest or work for it" to be included in it, obviously it is just here and we are here and coexisting with it- some would say within it or it within us! There is a great saying *"In Lacesh" which means the divine in me bows to the divine in you- But also there is nothing wrong with the Reiki tradition and it is humble yet pronounced and this is the best because it is needed and we have to be made aware of it/what we need for sure. I am proud to be such a one person who exposes people to the way of Reiki-

I pray we get more fascinated with things like that. Reiki is a stable foundation on which to live and have our being and it is as I mentioned earlier is not a problem or potential problem creator like some other traditions may seem like- it has nothing hidden in it accept for the information only for certain classes like the symbols and it is infinite like us and we can see how it is our friend forever! The dutiful nature we sometimes forgo is solidly found in how we are supported and encouraged in the Tradition of Reiki! I feel I am being called to teach others as my students, attuning them and preparing them to share in the Reiki energy with more people, lands, and animals of the Earth and all... I am located here in Buffalo, NY and I am starting to see that people may be desiring this and they may feel ready for this next step in their life. The biggest issue I take with people is some ways they disrespect the Reiki practice. This is not a very good choice, do not disrespect the person who may be responsible for healing you and all you have come in contact with.

I understand that as an empath I am trained in the art of dealing with darkness and that is not the fault of anyone but we also must use our loving awareness to become allies with those that are here for the selfless service of all beings in the cosmos, which is a Reiki healer.

The other issue I struggle with from time to time is the issue with charging people money for Reiki sessions. I believe that it is an art form and is deserving of payment! I believe that it is not about the payment, it is about the joy of living in alignment with divine wisdom and source energy and sending it out into the energy field around you assisting others on all levels.

This should help make it clear for you, humanity. Reiki is REAL. It is the white Light of God that, when seen through a crystal lens creates all forms are colors. It is powerful and wise. The Reiki itself is conscious and alive, it may not be alive in the same sense that a deer is but it is more like LIFE itself. Then we see that the true Reiki practitioner does not direct the energy as much as the Lord does and the Reiki moves through the practitioner, using them for its divine healing purposes. This is not scary, it is enlightening and ultimately extremely helpful and humbling. I believe that Reiki is not something we can categorize or predict. For example, I have given several sessions and more will come in the future, perhaps the near future, in which I have seen all kinds of lovely and powerful healings occur. The people respond differently to it, it is not something you can say- " this is how it will play out for you"... it is unpredictable in that sense, but I have faith that it is doing exactly what it should and what it is designed for that specific individual at that time in their life.

Sometimes it is very subtle and almost non-existent, and other times it is very obvious causing them to release huge emotional blockages. I feel that Reiki, just like God, does not waste energy or time. The Reiki moves into the person it is healing through the healer and even though the healer will follow some guidelines- the healing, just like life circumstances, are bound to change, do not fight this, flow with this. You will find it much easier and enjoyable for all involved. When I went into my Reiki level 2 class and attunement my teacher was calling on us to practice sending healing to another and she said that for me "I could handle multiple recipients at once."

The Reiki flows through some people more vigorously than others and there are many factors involved with this, but I believe that because my general sense of ego is surrender I allow the Reiki in deep trust, love, and gratitude to flow fully through me. I was discussing Reiki with a co-worker after he inquired and I told him that Reiki does not require anything of the recipient, which for some odd reason is strange and difficult for people to accept. You are here to receive healing energy, that's it. You do not have to believe anything, you do not have to breathe in a certain way, you do not have to say a billion prayers or close your eyes.

The Reiki energy is willing to commune with you and it is ultimately an expression of God, and the way I would describe it is the white light of creation. Its agenda is peace. It is simple. Peace that is actual and is based in the ultimate reality does not need to be summoned or manifested or forced into creation, it is creation in its most simplest form. This is the hope for humanity through Reiki healing. It does have some precepts but in no way is it a belief system, it is a lifestyle choice that promotes peace. Very simple.

It protects the recipient so that they feel safe enough to release and accept whatever they weren't accepting. It is in alignment with Talk Therapy by this way very clearly to remedy any confusion – the Truth of healing is that it is All One- Truth! So you can see clearer that way which is what Zen is all about!

I am hoping soon I can begin conducting formal classes because I am certified to do so; I have attained my Reiki level 3 master and teacher qualification. So, the way the levels of Reiki works is three fold. There are 3 distinct levels for some specific reasons, I am sure. The first level is for the purpose of self-healing. The student is educated on their own energy body that heretofore might have been quite a mystery to them. Then, at the end, usually, of the class after they have received the proper visual aids of the chakra system, the master attunes them with the Reiki energy. This is the shaking of the hands of the individual soul and the eternal Reiki energy who will come to be friends and form bonds into eternity.

There are certain steps for this and sometimes a crystal and prayers are involved in this important and holy process. Then eventually the student will return some time later for the next class.

After one or several months the student will return for the second class and attunement. They learn symbols and they learn how to use the energy to heal others. There is another attunement and more visual aids. The last level is the master teacher Level.

Many practitioners stop here and they only want to be healers rather than teachers of Reiki and join the lineage of masters into eternity. I chose the latter. In this final (?) class the students essentially move from being students to masters. They learn a few more symbols and they receive their final attunement in which the Reiki is now flowing through them without resistance or self-doubt. They now move through the world fully empowered by this mystical white light energy and assist humanity and beyond.

So, I believe if and when I get more clients I shall keep a journal of all of these sessions. I offer a free trial session like how at Guitar center we offer a kickstart, which is a 30 minute free trial one on one music lesson.

This is the same premise, you get to test it out with no cost to you besides your open mind and some of your time. I have noticed from one of my friends who was skeptical that after the session he felt the need to cry quite strongly.

This is a great sign of the reality of this healing potential. I believe that Reiki is something that goes deeper than our mind stuff. For example, when I am giving a session to someone I would often have conversations prior to or during the actual session, which may not be popular with other healers, it's an intuitive choice you can make for yourself based on what you feel from your client.

What I have noticed is that the benevolence and desire for complete healing and well-being of everyone that is the core of Reiki doesn't care what religion you are or really even how you view Reiki itself. This is essentially the absence of the darkness. The pure light of creation moving through Reiki healers is exactly what we need on the planet now. As I may have mentioned earlier in this book, the greatest Power requires the lightest touch. What this means can be explained with Reiki… Reiki can blast open a heart chakra with one touch if that is what God desires.

Reiki can move seamlessly throughout time and space and heal mysterious ancestral wounds that were still plaguing the present family lineage. Each symbol, which I do not want to openly mention here, all have their own purpose. There is one in particular that is used for this distance healing that also can be used to heal ancient wounds as I just explained.

The Rei-Ki lineage is understood through * Dr. Mikao Usui, in my perspective. There are other schools like Karuna, Tummo, and Holy Fire etc. Dr. Usui was a Buddhist monk who felt the pull of healing for all and he prayed and fasted for twenty one days alone. He was given the divine wisdom and insight of Reiki energy healing and how to heal people with this. The Reiki energy is reaching out to you, will you shake its hand? *Om Nam Myoho Renge Kyoho… "I am upholding the cosmic law" . Amen.

I share a lot, technically this entire book, from my personal experience. I recognize the relationship we have with Reiki is both objective and subjective and allows for more flow of energy, and as we know from the name of Reiki is Universal! The understanding a true Master has is so useful to the greatly demanded healing process- There are so many reasons and the most easily worded one is Confidence- is the ability to be seen and it is a special seeing! The vision I hold for everyone says the master's heart is benevolent! I sometimes may fall short but consistently I am wishing well to everyone consciously and this is my way of self-mastery just like thee Ascended Masters*. I honor each individual perspective on thee Earth for it is never frozen but flowing like the Energies. We are able of such destruction and despair, destruction is the external hell and despair is the internal hell. May thee acceptance of the true masters in conscious recognition of how life already is foster in us all a growth and begin the demise of Mara; the root of unnecessary suffering! I have an entire book on this called "The Reiki Bible: A Guide to Reiki Living" and a video I made in Instagram called "How Reiki is for Everyone"

Two LOG OF MEDIA entry's above- My book and video*

People most likely in China- practicing/ learning Tai Chi Qi Gong. I practice do you?

42
MARTIAL ARTS

I feel very excited to write some words on this one…

I believe that the martial arts serve a divine purpose. They can connect us to our deeper self and to God, but as with anything, it is up to us to choose an intention for our energetic expression. So, I believe that the martial arts is not actually meant to cause suffering even though we seem to see it on its surface as delivering blows, strikes, and defending from attackers. But in reality it can be used to soften the violence latent in our hearts and souls. We can, like I said, direct our intention and thus our minds energy to a positive experience that can be lighter. In fact that is the main thing with ALL MARTIAL ARTS- DIRECTION!

The way this is done is first respecting the tradition, exploring it and its history if that is what is exciting to you at this time. Then you may begin working with it within your own form.

> This means you begin to allow the apparent foreign path of eastern spirituality and physical expression that blurs the lines between dance and fighting to be a friend unto you.

The same way that God will come to you wherever you are, in any level of awareness or pain or pleasure, or emptiness, God loves us so much that God does not care what path you so choose to seek the ultimate Truth within. But I feel that God would prefer us to release our judgements towards others' choices. So, I mean by that try not to unconsciously suffer or attempt to make others suffer… because of their deviations from what YOU perceive as correct and normal.

The basis of all martial arts is the symbol of the ying yang. This symbol is wise and it has much to tell you.

The black within the white, the white within the black. What can I take from this to assist me and others? I can see that, I can FEEL that there is a serenity within the acceptance of the ying yang. When we move through existence we can be surprised if we are willing to experience differently we can use the wisdom of the Tao and of the Ying Yang for that specific and divine purpose; serenity. In reality, we are just seeking serenity most of the time.

I was just watching a TV show and there were 4 women, 2 the hosts, 2 the guests. The guests were speaking in support of medical marijuana (Cannabis) being used for healing. They went on to say that the women clientele were mostly interested in healing their sleep patterns, anxieties, and sexual energies. This is something that is aided greatly by the inclusion of the wisdom of the far east. I highly recommend the beautiful and mostly silent practice of Tai Chi Qi Gong in combination with therapy and a general acceptance of one's own perfect nature. The reason I consciously decided just then to use the adjective "perfect" is because it will cut out the need for us to perpetuate self judgements.

The reason we have some imbalances in America is because we strive too much. There is a lot to be learned from foreign cultures and, in reality, we are all from Africa, in an anthropological perspective. Perhaps I will also write about that later.

I can speak of my experience with Tai Chi practice as a means of communing with the love of God. I went to a class that cost some money and I noticed there wasn't a proper way of enjoyment for me. I believe that it is less about the memorization of the katas or movements and more focus should be upon the experience itself, for its own sake. For example, when we go into a meditative state we are essentially surrendering to the Tao. When we allow energy to flow through us uninterrupted we are using the wisdom of the Ying Yang properly. This is why yoga and Tai Chi are not necessarily competitive. They are bridges between you and God.

There must be a reason why watching a woman engage in tai Chi is so arousing to me. I feel that the discipline and focus is very powerful and attractive. The direct nature of it all is enjoyable and simple. The reason I stay away from most women is because there is a lack of direct communication, at least in my age group. I believe that there is a purity in the authenticity of a disciplined woman who is not afraid to be both strong and gentle; to be both yin and yang. She is accepting all of herself in her heart and soul.

She is choosing to steer her soul towards the infinite bliss of the Lord God. She is aware of herself and improves everyday. She is blissful. She is aware. She is love- living, walking, and breathing on this Earth. So divine. She may transcend the need for purpose soon. She may awaken to her own inner light and then she will be free, ultimately. This is my hope and my joy.

Every man, woman and child is spending and receiving energy. It is only right that we learn to adapt and to harness this energy fully to make our way through the day with a lightness of Heart and presence of soul. We may believe many things but we will all be one in the stillness and in that Peace of the universe and its will.

Instead of talking about all of the steps involved in the spiritual practice of Tai Chi, physically speaking, I decided to follow my bliss in my heart and write with passion.

MY passion! I feel the burning away of illusions and the coming up of peace in me when I practice. I feel the acceptance of myself as a prayer in a divine moment. I have said Tai Chi is like praying with your body- this I believe.

I just did a Tai Chi class that was much less stressful than a paid class. Perhaps it doesn't matter if your form is correct all the time. I, reflecting on that experience, was glad to be participating and sharing the space with mostly women. This is important because I am a Leo! I enjoy spending time with them a lot! It also is good for an energetic reason, I feel that I sometimes have a lot of testosterone or masculinity and I sometimes need women, a lot of them, to have that balance. I feel the Lord as Love wants us to flow our energy fully.

I believe that when we resonate with this sense of freedom from everything we can be heard, and feel validated and enjoy who we are made to be. I wish for trust to abide, I feel sometimes sad and need to be seen and heard fully, this is in direct relationship with God's Love and wisdom and discipline. When we know our own needs we can allow the meeting of those to come to fruition.

BUT it takes courage to allow that to be okay with you first and then other people will follow. You need to be willing to take care of yourself before you can trust someone else to "take care" of you too. And that is, I suppose, part of this Tai Chi Qi Gong in the way that God knows what we need and what we want before we think it up. What I am saying is the energetic experience of Tai Chi Qi Gong is as follows,

> the hand moves as a cloud moves, the other hand follows suit, and you breathe. The movement between self and other is witnessed and fully expressed.

So, when we choose to trust in our own divine intimacy we move toward goals with undaunted charisma and drive. This is the intrepid state of pure awareness of Self. God did not make a mistake here, your desires are not wrong, in the least, at all, period, end of sentence. I believe that this generation of unprecedented awareness, through spiritual exercises like Tai Chi, is necessary for us; it gives routine to hold onto to the way God is holding on to us, so subtly and yet so powerfully.

We can move with trust in that process. I feel that the wonder of all of this is we think that God belongs to all of us, not just the Christians, the Buddhists at Pine Bush NY know this in some ways, they follow to the best of their ability the way of *Thich Nhat Hanh, a Vietnamese buddhist who has a relationship with God within the emptiness of Buddha. There is so much to learn from these ancient practices a lot of which is available through their collective and historical artwork. I feel that because I have deep emotions that moving with awareness and deep breathing in prayer like ways opens up these hidden caverns. I feel that the needs of my body and soul and heart are coming to be seen as pure and holy within my own heart and I am willing to be vulnerable.

This is the cultivation and divine practice of Self-honesty. I have confessed things before and I am getting tired of it, I would rather "confess" or rather discuss these ideas of "sin" toward my trusted friends, rather than be hurt by a priest, which is really just a robe to them. Jesus is a priest in the order of Melchizedek as it says in that book, there is a part of our new age experience or movement that is deeply reminiscent of this Melchizedek way. It is completely lacking in judgement between the light and darkness as God himself is. This sets priorities straight that have been perverted beyond recognition throughout Earth's interesting history and evolution processes.

As I believe God wants us to use our own mind to distinguish between order and chaos this is our only hope, and in the end, I love you! So, If Jesus was truly in alignment with divinity and Truth he knows that Truth that *Drunvalo Melchizedek lives in and as also. I believe Drunvalo Melchizedek should be our judge, if anyone is. He is an absolutely beautiful man who deserves to be heard, seen, felt, and adored for his commitment to the ancient ways of perfected Love; the Illuminated Heart!

The way all these "religions" are different yet work together as One is here in this excerpt, I'll prove it now!

I went to Tai Chi and I felt anger and it was very clear. I went to a new place down the street and felt the culmination of this adversity and my seemingly powerless state to move the mountains of my emotional body, until I let it out! I hereby release you, emotion, into this book as words of truth and divine healing wisdom! Be free! Do you see what I am saying? This Tai Chi moved my blockages through me and it was difficult as true healing is and then it came out into this book through my laptop for the greater good of humanity at large! Thank you Tai Chi Qi Gong…

If you were a person I would hug you so tight and then release you forever. As we all do, every moment, with every breath. Ram Ram. Peace be with you. May the great Truth of peace abide within you!

On a side note:

The martial Arts is meant to be a removal process as well for our ego. The children who are so inclined may practice and hone their skills of what is called the "hard" martial arts styles and forms first. *These are Tae Kwon Do, Karate, and Muay Thai… then kung fu or wushu is a bridge between the hard and soft styles and forms for one very specific reason. It is channeling animals and their valuable natures. But, a snake can strike and it can also coil. A crane can spread its wings and fly yet it also can fold its legs inward and reflect. So, the tiger can and will prowl but beware of its sharp and hard claws and teeth.

This is too difficult for a lot of older people so they all do the soft tai Chi, Aikido, and mindfulness movements. So, I skipped some grades and I practiced Tai Chi without mastering any other forms besides generally being mindful. I may benefit greatly from Wushu! I am perpetually obsessed with Martial Arts films, one of my favorite is* "The Quest" with Jean Claude Van Damme, Some of the others are "Mortal Kombat", "Street Fighter 1 and 2" also with Jean Claude Van Damme, and who could skip "Cyborg", then there are the more traditional less comical or animated based films like "Ip Man" with Donnie Yen and "The Last Samurai" with

Tom Cruise. The lists go on and on because Martial Arts is fun and relevant as long as we have bodies and even then we can see that with names like "cloud hands" you can emulate the clouds with your hands as if you were on the tippy top of the mountain peak.

The benefit of the soft martial Arts is very obvious in the name of the Japanese one; Aikido. Ai-ki-do translates approximately to the way of peace and harmony. The reason this is an accurate title is because if you watch someone like *Steven Seagull, who seems to be quite practiced in this form, it is extremely rare that any Aikido master will start a fight or will throw any strikes, their only purpose is to show the adversary where they are falling short of inner tranquility and perfected balance. This relies on self-awareness, mindful choices and the quick reflex to move the opponent with their own misplaced energy. LOG OF MEDIA- VIDEO – AIKIDO*

This is acting as a revolving door and is actually a form of perfect mercy because they are not inflicting damage; they are only maintaining Peace in their community, which seems to be wherever they are presently. This is essential for Police officers because it is in their job title, "peace officer"… In LA they started a meditation group for the police there, I have been saying to my Dad for years "All the cops should be Zen monks!" * LOG OF MEDIA- VIDEO; police incorporate meditation.

43
SEXUALITY

The topic at hand is very sensitive. We all are familiar with sexuality as it is. I am writing this book for a big reason; to reveal the power of LoVE!

I believe the sexual energy is divine or, to be accurate, is destined to merge one with divinity. The actual sexual pull or energy is different than the physical realization or manifestation of sex. I am a very sexual being and I feel that the energy is overly dismissed by society. Let me extrapolate; the desire to merge is actually quite serious. This feeling of a craving for the body of another also is not specifically sexual always.

I wouldn't mind if I could actually hug or hold a woman ~ That is all. For example, if there was a woman that was abandoned as a child I could hold her for a night. I would not be offended if she felt sexual or did not at all ~ and the same for myself that night. I know of the raw potential for sexual and creative energy. We do not want to fracture this energy, we want to be direct with it. This is important because when we are in desire we should trust that our energy body is not wrong.

This is a self-Loving practice.

When we decide how to adopt our own sexuality we cherish it and embrace it into our heart. So, if we actually communicate what we feel and also what we want we will be moving in the right energetic direction.

My opinion on sexuality, as with all things, is based in energy. The energy itself is in order or is moving towards being in order. This is not quite OCD, or overly obsessive, and by the way I believe that mental fascinations like that are based in a soul desire for actual Truth and order. The intensity is experienced as real because on an energetic level it is literally the energy of God, creation, or Reality being expressed and experienced AND dealt with within you as a human being, it is a holy gift, be grateful for it.

The energy of creation is at hand in this divine sexually engulfed moment. You are freedom and the energy is basically you. This is something to be enjoyed and when it flows properly it allows us to be more in alignment. I do not know everything in reference to sexuality but I do know the Love that I possess for you, forever and ever.

The basics of sexuality to foster growth and healing are based in ~Light~. When we are honest we feel better and we are portraying ourself to the world, our true self.

Then we may be cherished and admired for who we are. When we see ourself as not separate from the lakes and rivers we begin to understand a deeper respect for the Earth, our Home. And when we see ourself in the stars shining we understand our true flawless expanse and grandeur. The real desire of sexual impulse, I pray, should be met by the authentic Love we all have access to, always, not denied, abandoned, or consistently rejected. The Heart understands, accepts, and abides.

I believe the desire to please another, so that they are completely satisfied is an aspect of the divine. And when we see the other person as ourself we are basically fully understanding the completion process of Love, the full circle and remembrance.

Sexuality

I feel the fear, guilt, and shame that has plagued our hearts shall end, soon. I know that the energy writing these words is so in Love with you! I believe that my heart may want to share itself with you now. I do not feel ashamed or burdened to be open for you! I love, and that is that. When someone blesses you they bless ALL of who you are. When someone states "I love you" it means the entire context of your being and experience on ALL levels.

The experience of Reiki energy has allowed me to blossom and fully embody my own sexuality. I feel the lack of self-hate and aspect of completion has basically connected my heart with the heart of God. And the love, joy, and fulfillment know no bounds. You deserve a good hug and a wet kiss. Sri Ram.

Instead of giving you the same energy of this book in so many words over and over again like a sexual feeling and motions... ehem* I instead – instead, uhuh,, yep … mmm , mhm, yes Love, yes dear soul! Want to give you a memory of how you were when first imagined sex and how opening and free you must have been- like it was something like a breeze that crossed your new face upon the old Earth, Yahweh, what a sound God's name it resounds. So, the beginning of everything, new life, has to start somewhere it starts right where we all have had this experience- this MEMORY. I am so special says all life everywhere no matter what! I just want you to feel good and be caressing rather than judging or demeaning says thee author and all the angels- first perhaps we can clarify first? Why is that first?

> Because if you want to get better at sex or be the best knowing yourself and knowing another is all about your foundation in your mind- How YOU alone perceive.

The other people though they can be positive and supportive you being in charge of yourself is what makes other souls less afraid of being in charge of themselves! Inside of you and outside of you again and again- it is like meditation practice and then when you are done being inside yourself!

I feel it is so good to be aware of more and more and to not segregate your sexuality from that- to grow and to learn and be more at Peace and not struggle with your situation of having a moon and a Sun and an Earth to be around us- So, as I said- I just want to give you myself like a bed to lay on not a challenge in me about everything you are and claim to be... To be like a watery bed that you can fully have your skin on. And just knowing I am around like a hug that is somehow never too tight – but when you exhale I'm always so desperate to smell your breath and to give way hopefully with you in tandem to my passions The simplicity of Life is further present in this sacred sexuality and you never need be impressive to me says Life but knowing that the Stars and the moon are mine and I will hold on to them while you allow that lower area to beholden you and know more about that room than anything else in all of my Creation, for I am God! The lower region of the other is never yours but yet we feel we want to connect it... !

44
MENTAL CONDITIONS OR ALTERED PERSPECTIVES

I am not so unfamiliar with this quite unique personal experiences that fall under this category of life and the mind/brain. My mother is a psychologist. I have been exposed to western medicine/pills. And I have felt the immense pressure to succeed and be somehow different~ This is the negative side of an altered mind perspective, or rather the society's response to this varied viewpoint or experience of life.

I believe that the brain has unlimited potential for experience of life. This means that our "familiar" territory is only that, the mental space in which we have remained in. The ability for us to see life in a way that is utterly and fully our own is mostly disregarded. I exist to share the wisdom of unlimited heart and cosmic mind to you. I also feel the joy of building confidence for you.

To me, the greatest healing possible for those who are experiencing life differently from a mental standpoint is immense understanding from another. Fulfill their needs, feed them, clothe them, wash them, help them to find release, relaxation, and repose… AND divine purpose, we all have one, trust me. The desires they have are not different than yours, you can help them with that at least. And then realize in deep humility the similarities and contemplate the differences.

The experience of pressure from an energetic vantage point creates another system that requires releasing. When there is too much pressure in a pipe it can burst. When we are not understanding we can cause harm. To be willing to heal is always the first step. In my experience, personally, I have noticed the reason or motivation for my potential insanity is because of a lack of worthiness for my own being-ness. I felt that I was being filtered through a lens of immense disillusionment and comparison.

I had a breakdown. I knew what was happening and I understood the way it seemed. I did not care. I wish that people were free from the mental constructs and could be at peace in complete serenity and emptiness. In that space they find self-worth and a desire to be happy once more. When we look at the positive perspective of mental conditions and altered perspectives we encounter differing levels of genius and superpowers.

The manic depressive state of *Jimi Hendrix, the genius nature and mind powers of savants or Autistics. We find the understanding peeking through their eyes. They want to understand us too, and in reality, the apparent differences between those with an altered perspective and us who do not experience that so much should shift, naturally. My desire for all is to realize and honor balance.

Something worth mentioning is Shamanic perspective. The indigenous cultures have an archetype known as the medicine man, or the shaman that works in altered states of consciousness which some of these people who seem quite out of it may be interacting with on a day to day basis.

They believe that schizophrenia is actually shaman sickness or the initiation for one to work as a shamanic healer! I worked with Autistic children for several months. I do not regret it. The children are spectacular but the adults lack understanding from time to time. WE find that the foundation for our actions must be held in a clear light of awareness. We must not ignore ourselves especially when we are around children. The energy body has an innate intelligence that supersedes and supervises our limited perspectives. The energy we sense and feel is working to attuning us to each other's hearts, for the greater good of everyone. What we must come to understand is that our idea of right and wrong is not based in reality if it is consistently harming children.

The basic instructions I have for adults pertaining to children, and in this excerpt, for Autistic or any other "different" kids is thus: ~Approach them with sincere humility.~ Do not demand things of them. Just because they have an altered perspective does not put you in charge of them, ever. You are barely in charge of yourselves. These children are not interested in being harmed or causing harm to you or anyone else. They have a way of moving through life that is needed. This is why God has used them here on Earth. As I have come to know it,* "when the power of love overcomes the love for power, the world will know peace" - Jimi Hendrix. This world is part of a grand existence! You are so much more powerful and beautiful than you make yourself out to be. The only way for us to learn and evolve is with and through consistent humility and discipline. God knows what we need and want, the children, and especially, the 'different" ones are basically here for that exact purpose.

Trust me. If you see them as actually able to teach you, you will learn something new and blessed from them. I do love you and I do know what I am talking about. May your perspective be blessed with zen waves of clarity! Enjoy your mind and your life.

*LOG OF MEDIA - VIDEO "Proper Perspective on Mental Health" by Joe Vertino (Author) from Youtube channel!

... This Video exemplifies a steady individual who happens to be me thee author. I am in love with myself. A point I make in this divinely inspired video- with a clear mind- is the proper perspective on the (human) mind! The mind is beautiful and further it is MEANT TO BE. It has a natural "Pull towards God" as I mentioned early in my work; a chapter title, itself. The mind without being interfered with has a desire to literally grow up- into higher "planes" of consciousness- simply this means scientifically we are accessing the grander way to BE CONSCIOUS. And (in science) we have an understanding of the brain and its coherence with all of our (possible) perceptions. This great language is literally called higher brain- the lower, mid, and higher brain. And that we are not limited to one part of our brain. We have such an easier time without inhibiting as we say in Hinduism even though I Am a Zen Buddhist, the obstacles and blockages whether intentional or not- are simply the only deterrent to our proper access to our own birthright of consciousness in perpetuity- which implies time and space and thus EVOLUTION. The reference to Hinduism is Lord Ganesha "the remover of Obstacles"

The divine is something as you incline your current contemporary self- because of the great love that pervades there is a benevolence and a goodness that does not cause one to panic or worry - which if someone was reading this could become like which is why I mention. Even the name; "Allah" seems to convey it in the most poetic way- which is undeniable truthful poetry, honest like trees on our Earth. The natural responses to our environment are the beginning, a clear word called authenticity is it. That is what make sense as the beginning place of true evolution- and as you begin here your journey is inevitably actual- mental illness we can say, obviously, is based in the sometimes almost complete denial of the same thing we are authentic about; generally Life Universally.

And mental illness is the "mis-use" of the brain- as we mentioned earlier comes from potential regressive influence from others - through their own lies and deceit towards, whether intentional or not, YOU (most likely?) in childhood- if the case is the worst possible- sexual and etc. abuse by parent.

The dharma of us ALL :) Is (always) to learn- and I am elated to exclaim you are doing your dharma right here and now guaranteed.

"The seeds of the Earth are able to be laced down and after we have planted them we can simply walk away and know in stillness or in play that there is nothing to worry about, about our seeds and our eventual food."

This idea ;

IS, appropriate to perpetuate like the Light of the Sun in our generations onward and upward, a.k.a. our children!

The general needs don't close off like a broken pipe - they are stuck- unlike the litter on our streets and even the politicians in their office!

These needs therefore are more foundational than both of those, politicians and litter and it is necessary to acclimatize to what is certain and even is our true measure and God's inescapable mark upon us ALL.

So your dharma is naturally to perpetuate ourself and we cannot help but understand our dharma externally to help creation prosper, individually alone, is bound to our (optimized) health and healing agenda!

It is ok to let go of both the litter and politics and to simply be put to thee Earth- to be more accurate with your rear-end. Sometimes the only good thing we can do for everyone is to do not a one- and in context of this chapter is to not attempt to fix the broken parts of yourself any further or parts of anything in any of the possible worlds but to remain broken, some people who are good at being still called meditators, would say remain broken as long as possibly can and let things also get broken and then retain their free will the agenda of the Universe – of all the worlds of you and me and freedom eventual rings. Especially if you do this and you may even fall in Love with me- it. It's called MEDITATION- it is the best thing ever… whisper whisper* until you are done and then meditation has begun. It is a break from the world and the world so to speak in which you have your mental illness… I love you that way and so does God honestly- if it makes you feel better to know that is also what is meant when people are following Jesus Christ and the narrow way- but ultimately it is a core of innocence that I aim to please and heal and save and protect and encourage and witness. But understand me; meditation is the best thing!

Steffany Gretzinger- awesome positive musical influence, amen.

45
MUSIC

Well, we all know Music! What about it do we really know? There are many angles to take- There is the objective truth and language we could use the simple terms "music theory" for. Then there is the subjective, which is the sometimes infinitely personal experience that is by definition incapable of being experienced by another. And then another angle is the wide open majority of swaying and crying out and yelling and dancing- which is the group experience which includes both- the audience.

We could also learn about a special perspective which is about the creation itself and the idea of creator and then the "job" of experiencing. There is specific intention always necessary for the music to be put into motion and actualized and then the experiencer is we could say also using their choice.

So, in that sense we have a self-declared formula.

"This is my work" says the creator of the music and then the audience goes "This is now my experience".

And the objective understanding that pervades a band and its performance is present before and during the performance, in fact the performance is bound to the (proper) use of the objective world of music and then the subjective experience is always inevitable of every person involved- but we could say and assert that the subjective experience of the audience is priority rather than the band's... and then we could attempt to fully understand that by understanding that the band has to *stay* in the realm of the objective and then they are "providing" the audience with the **stage** to experience the music on basically in whatever manner is seen fit by the audience into the future.

There is the cultural part; Culture is prior to the arising of music particularly in its objective realm, meaning the development of repeating patterns especially that can be communicated from one musician to another and repeated by them also.

Culture is something that is inevitable and by its nature remains after its formation. And I take a very reasonable approach to culture as it is. That culture is a consistency and is arising out of the specific region and its factors... the factors have a specific resonation and then culture forms basically. So, the factors are the weather/climate, animal life, plant life, sounds, landscape that are around the people and the people have to be in some kind of peaceful enough living situation where they are able to establish what is known as culture.

So, music... we could obviously say comes out of these factors BUT there is also the vantage point of inspiration that is seemingly arising out of nowhere or nothingness (of Love). The sounds being made from a person's mouth or the sound using a certain item can become a repeatable pattern as long as the motor skills are permitting.

Then something magical happens when the person transforms their perspective from one of simply arching and striking with their wrist while holding a stick onto a resonant surface and then it becomes a new thing!

Then I would assume the brain fires new synapses the soul resonates and we have the feeling of great excitement and that includes potential for a new creation- Music!

And Humanity became fascinated with this- and took it to what would seem like its end but then the transformation that occurred in the human when music happened (for the first time) occurred also in the music and then you have a what we could label a constant creation.

For some reason I think the musical composer Henry Purcell. * He is a genius he has many songs that I feel I can write about.

One is "An evening hymn"* VIDEO LOG OF MEDIA. I sang and performed this song in University. It was awesome. The now what we know as thee ART of music is so contemplative and subtle and then suddenly wild but controlled and professional and complete we could say. To have a discipline about something that we could say is seemingly so random and unfixed seems like a miracle! That it just came and then it stayed! And we fully capitalized on it and clutched to it and found solace and joy great seemingly unending joy inside it; Music.

I mentioned some more contemporary lyrics earlier in this great book and I am proud of myself. I feel the energy of musician's is something akin to that; pride! The word we usually hear or *use* is "eccentric." It pervades rather than closes down or pinches off. And it can be severely intimidating. Thee profession of Music is a very important field and has deep roots and I understand that inherently but I am not everyone.

Thee Earth is its home and a civilized base of communal life is its fertile soil if we remember…

So, and the natural way of humankind has its breath and its relief. I think of *Bobby McFerrin who WAS A MEDICINE MAN. Zeene Weene Boo Woahp Zoap! He was brilliant and would do his dharma on the stage and in the music hall with the orchestra and without some shoes on, and with his dreads tied and with the conducting stick in his hand(s).

"If Music be the food of Love sing on sing on, sing on sing on, til I am filled and filled with joy." - which is from Henry Purcell. *

One more point: You may notice that at events they will always have music regardless of the reason for the coming together. *"God spoke and light was made" The speaking is like music, the sound.

> A Poem: "Thee Angels giving way to Humanity's Plight"
>
> I bet when angels speak to God it is like Music perhaps to some humans if we could hear it- and music is so vast in its scope it covers all the lands and fills the soul with pleasure for it all it can accomplish with or without our hands involved in its doing nature… it is.. that way… forever?

The music letting it win. Letting us see the waves when on the beach. And when we look lovingly at the waves we are readying ourself to perceive properly. To convince yourself in the presence of angels alone that you can release the maladaptive behavior in yourself that climbed on you when you were younger when you felt sick in the head like vines climbing up a wall. But your wall was only meant to convey something to help you not to truly block anything out or keep anything in even. The divine I AM knows it is said in your heart- "you are still starring perhaps starry eyed by now at the waves- you know by now you don't get to control the waves! And don't you want to properly perceive? Kid."

This agenda-less scene of the watery birth of each crescent is perhaps nothing to the Lord but that you are there at the beach. The joy of devotion comes from that. Ah knowledge still exists in the libraries there is nothing to be afraid of with devotion in little bits.

This silence does call us into itself somehow with the waves going and the Lord watching and the swelling of my own watery current of my personal Life- why would SILENCE win out? Over truly over and against deathly hallows could win?

How epic. Like The Odyssey who knows you not especially if it a track, you listen to me, if it is a track like in Christmas with the cars and you have to do WHAT?! Enter and exit the cars you are not the cars or the track…

So with all this commotion and convincing natures even the sounds of deep unto deep music and great worship and prayer never in jest because it is honest work to save souls unknown- MUSIC... calls unto SILENCE... surrenders itself willingly or unwillingly into its arms of grace for grace is all around and God has never hid from anyone! So is it even possible to ruin the surprise as someone who has gone into SILENCE or is it a wash, haha, might as well take off your clothes and walk in lovingly and eventually exit the waves -there there.

The waves will be there and have been from before we were born in human form- but MUSIC the food of Love is such a visceral and palpable relationship that God certainly uses- unlike the waves- and awake as we are still there is such a calling for the herd and us lonely sheep in Music's deep reverent way, for reverence is the most important thing. The swell of you is holy! At least remember that.

Archangel Sandalphon- the one of Music - bless us all.

46
HONOR: (MUST READ)

Quite a mysterious experience for many westerners. Honor is a great sounding word. It is simple and straightforward. We often mistake honor for its companions like integrity, grit, wisdom, and perseverance. But I believe it is a different word for a special purpose. Honor is connected to the root of Reiki wisdom. The real Reiki masters live in a constant state of honor and act as leaders for the village. The Reiki healer knows what life does to people because it is literally ALL of their divine business as the healers, energetically.

Why is honor important? Honor is a linchpin for society to move into a more authentic yet suitable way of processing its experiences both individually and communally/collectively- but yet moving forward is an illusion in context – progression is a potentially insulting to thee truly honorable human- it is confusing for some reason! The impulse to move forward through Life of others is not my business and why would I want to progress with them? Why would I need to- rather let's look at that in the face- am I dependent on them? Do they pull my chains? Do I pull theirs if so I am still! I am at least not insulting to myself and to the clouds!

I am shining says the Sun and I am not afraid of that human and his eyes as he doesn't think about other things than myself- is that Honor Lord God who created me? asks the Sun about the Human. I am still and contemplating honor and it seems wrong sometimes these movements I could make in this our shared world. I am destined- what a ring that sentence has in me! I am destined I have purpose and as I get up and make movements my purpose drives me. I can know that these honorable movements in myself are forever- so when I lay down I lay down happier and I am surrendered and eventually this surrender I can say becomes more and more of being-

Nirvana... eventually! This is why Reiki came from a Samurai who then became a Buddhist Monk!

Honor is a way of sitting, when someone is filled with honor they put it into everything they attempt and accomplish. Honor can bring someone through horrible experiences seemingly unscathed. And, reversely, when people don't understand the vibration or frequency of honor they fall apart at their seams because they don't know their creator. So, why does that matter? If you want to be able to move swimmingly through experiences then study the honor of Reiki.

When someone knows this they are stable beyond life and death, in their soul. Honor, just like Reiki, can carry on from one incarnation to the following ones. So, when people are in a pickle they are all alone and they have to make decisions on that alone. The only way to know you are moving correctly is by being in honor. The best relationship is the one surrounded with honor. When a couple of people grow in love together they can accomplish anything that cannot be destroyed by anyone unless the Lord wishes it so- the same Lord who commands Lord Buddha.

Google: honor: "high respect; great esteem". This definition is somewhat accurate. But Honor is not so much in reference to a subject and an object though, this is why I said "somewhat". Real honor does not have an honorer and an honoree, it is for its own sake as all things should be, if peace is to reign properly! Being honorable is what promotes civility from the inside out! Walking down a street with honor can make all of the darkness vanish, when someone is in that place, they are intrepid; they are the ground, the feet, the breath, the air, the people. Honor can connect us in Oneness. It is based in respect but it also works in tandem with the actual Truth.

When people are One they have "self" Love for everyone! I feel such a relief in discussing this! I believe that the opposite of honor is doubt and shame... for example, the mind can bring peace into itself when there is proper honor in life and death, equally, this comes back to balance! There is a reality that observes all experiences. When we see this we move with honor. We can feel a simple bliss that is beyond our understanding. This is affectionately referred to as the Lord of hosts because God is our host! We are dining at the table of earthly delights, being many experiences in varying intensities, and God is our invisible host, perpetually available because Love never dies.

Honor is also relevant to all beings. If we have free will we have honor available to us, ever accessible.

So, honor allows regrets to be eliminated. When someone must die they die fully and completely, with one strike. When someone must heal they heal fully, softly or quickly. When someone pauses they stop and sit and enjoy the nothingness aspect of God perhaps that will show up on their path today- a great grace that produces understanding. But this is a zenith... when there is Zen there is the zenith the singularity point. Where all is joy. And bliss.

And, when someone makes love, they enjoy it.

When someone is a master they can only attain true mastery with divine honor to balance out all aspects. In the 10 commandments of the Bible it says "Honor the mother and father". This is a good commandment. The reality of honor holds things together like the glue for arts and crafts. The honor must shine forth; it cannot be hidden. When this is seen it should encourage honor latent in others who see it to grow and become prevalent. The connection to Reiki is so simple when A student learns it they learn self-healing first and then they learn healing for others who is preferably their immediate family and then others outside of that and eventually can teach it as a master- and what is not clear about the similarity in healing and honor for our mother and father as in the Bible quote?

The positive works this way, the negative in some clear ways is different... I prefer *Bashar's (Darryl Anka's soul connection) definitions of positive and negative energies for its simplicity. Negative energy segregates and divides and positive energy includes. This is why I have so much Love because it is the bridge for the unconscious decisions made in darkness to come into the Light of God and pure joy.

This is a perpetual process in one way but it is also an actual process in another way. Here is a video of the thee aspects of both positive and negative objectively- one good reason as a Reiki master Healer as to why is we are living in a shared universe called objective reality and we ALWAYS have an inevitable subjectivity and positivity is something that is able to heal "us" because it is not generating in anyway the fear of sustained safety that is the ultimate simplicity and on which we can build complexity alone.

The patience and faith of leaders is what can accomplish this! The clarity and once again fearlessness of positivity is able to intellectually destroy negativity even without any attempt at communication – for example if there is one person on a park bench (like Eckhart Tolle was after his awakening) and this person is only sitting there alone BUT they are not having read my words perhaps and are struggling and clearly being and "choosing" negative rather than the same person choosing positive – so this person without doing or even attempting to communicate anything… is even if they are believing in something that may not be completely "rational" based on societal means currently, I mean we all know that society is in need of improvement and that judgement can be unhelpful and that judgment on a Park bench without any means or attempts to communicate is a completely unnecessary aspect of our cherished consciousness – the lack of judgement we can say should not come from exhaustion alone that would be the result of negativity. Positivity as I mentioned is not "afraid" of simplicity and you may notice just a tiny sliver of Truth- "I am afraid of allowing myself to be simple." And in that recognition you are choosing positivity and growth! "How delightful, says Mr. Sun – to have me met your face with myself; the rays… again today - … that bench!"

VIDEO LOG OF MEDIA – Bashar youtube video for positive and negative beliefs ! Highly Useful. *

The Earth for example is moving from a fear based planet to one of Love and Light. This is seen very clearly when you are keen and observant. This is, as I said, also a perpetual process. We move from experience to experience, dimension to dimension through the universe and its infinite loving awareness because it is our HOME. There is always more to heal and learn but not when it gives you a headache too much. Bashar also says that pain that cannot be understood by physical means is an indication of the true self suffering deeply. This means if we are in pain we are not allowing energy to flow as it is meant to. Sit with this. Process this. Feel …this… and breathe in God's Love. If this pain is not acknowledged it can cause disaster! And to make this chapter clear Honor is such a one that it brings up the awareness that you are ok and enables you to feel better and therefore make decisions that are not harmful to yourself or others!Like not being afraid if acknowledging hidden pains! It is the foundation of the Universal will of creation and what Enables expansion it is what we need- Honor!

Reiki Hugs.

CONCLUSION

This book is and was designed to create an energy field around you of pure Loving awareness which is your eternal birthright that you may have forgotten. I hope this helps you! I love you all. I want you to accept the things that have happened to you fully so that you may enjoy life abundantly. When we resist we are in denial- specifically of what and how powerful we really are. When we accept we are mature and becoming wise. I believe that the eternal reality is perfect in all aspects and you are part of that -being reminded of that now! I believe that this journey is beyond us yet it is IN us, forever. Melchizedek is a consciousness that is used by the Lord to move people up the evolutionary dimensional ladders into God's heart, which at some point when you get a headache you can just point to your own heart and be happy.

> Lord of Love, I pray that this power to create I am using properly. I pray I may be humble and may be wise and I pray we may find solace deep within these words. I pray we may surrender to the authenticity of our divinity. I thank you for giving us experience to behold. I thank you for all the different levels of consciousness and exercising of free will, I pray we may take it into our heart and breathe it and transmute the pain into Loving awareness. I pray we may rest and find peace. Amen.
> In honor of Ram Dass, Dr. Mikao Usui and the beloved Mother Mary thee Ascended master. Ram Ram. *
> Namaste.
> Peace be with you, your soul – and all the people you have met in this incarnation ;)

LOG OF MEDIA :

1. PAGE 12- Line 25 "The Nothingness of Love : A Buddhist book of Poetry by (same author) Joseph H. Vertino"- Available as of now as an E-book on amazon.com LINK: https://www.amazon.com/-/es/Joseph-H-Vertino-ebook/dp/B0CK2F2W2Q

2. Page 18- Line 3 Teal Swan video- thee Spiritual Catalyst: video title type in on youtube.com "What is Shadow work? - Teal Swan" https://www.youtube.com/watch?v=2s8I3yq-Kmo

3. Page 19-Line 3 – Video from The Musical Jesus Christ Super star (song is "Too Much Heaven on their Minds") type in on youtube.com: "Jesus Christ Superstar (1973) - Heaven on their minds" https://www.youtube.com/watch?v=URWa0rbB1Kw

4. Page 21- Line 28 Song by Lama Gyurme "Hope for Enlightenment" – type in on youtube.com "Lama Gyurme- Hope for Enlightenment" https://www.youtube.com/watch?v=VLyxJw89q2I

5. Page 23- Line 15- Author's Soundcloud – personally recorded music – type in on soundcloud.com : "Joe HV" will be guy with gray sweater and shades ⊠ "https://soundcloud.com/jvertino/open-the-eyes-of-my-heart

6. Page 45- Line 8- type in on youtube.com : "The Best of Mr. Rogers" Fred Rogers video : https://www.youtube.com/watch?v=mSbYQz-3rluM

7. Page 46- Line 15 – Type in on youtube.com: "Gangaji- The heart can bare it all" but if this doesn't come up there are many videos all of which are great! Gangaji – Spiritual guide video "The Heart can Bear it All" https://www.youtube.com/watch?v=49gB8r2W17E

8. Page 54- Line 19 Found on Instagram(.com) by user (type in) "andromedajoe811" name of video is "How Reiki is for Everyone" Author- Dr. Joe Vertino's video from his Instagram "How Reiki is

for Everyone" https://www.instagram.com/andromedajoe811/reel/DEDDM0wykND/

9. Page 55- Type in on youtube.com "How to Achieve Spiritual Balance- Rama" he has a special blue shirt you should see it. Line 17 Zen Master Rama video - https://www.youtube.com/watch?v=iC2-78GTGPs

10. Page 55- Line 40- Another book from Author – Type in on amazon.com "The Reform of the Education System by Joseph H. Vertino" Link here to author's website (strange name I know) "The Reform of the Education System" www.joevertino.org

11. Page 58- Line 13- type in on youtube.com "Heart Meditation By Drunvalo Melchizedek"- Video by Drunvalo Melchizedek link here (Heart Meditation – very good!) https://www.youtube.com/watch?v=mja7hKE-BC8

12. Page 59 – Line 22- Type in on youtube.com "Hildegard von Bingen- Canticles of Ecstasy" - Video music of Hildegaard von Bingen : https://www.youtube.com/watch?v=Ei88J4lERb-k&list=PL22P6-DEP1384IfNJE17tP-0Y-XBELUhN

13. Page 61 – Line 7 – Type in user name is on Tiktok is "jvertino" and name of video is "Connecting to thee Earth"- Link Video by Author on his Tiktok profile : "Connecting to thee Earth" https://www.tiktok.com/@jvertino/video/7335788819364531502

14. Page 64 – Line 3 – Video called "Self Love is the way Home" on youtube by author "Joe Vertino"(type in in search bar) (channel) - https://www.youtube.com/watch?v=QmwzfqLtRpM

15. Page 66- Line 31-Type in on youtube.com "Divine Laughter of Freedom – Mooji Clips"- Link for Mooji Baba- video of "Divine Laughter" youtube – important stuff-https://www.youtube.com/watch?v=bMIDSsDYV1M&t=321s

16. Page 67 – Line 24 – Youtube video "Awareness is not separation" by

author- channel name on youtube.com is "Joseph Vertino" – Link here https://www.youtube.com/watch?v=XJE549ARIq8

17. Page 75- Line 8 – Type in on youtube.com in search bar "The Great 14th : Tenzin Gyatso, the 14th Dalai Lama in his own words TRAILER" Link here VIDEO LOG OF MEDIA of Tenzin Gyatso ; https://www.youtube.com/watch?v=jDf7UJy9t8c

18. Page 77 – Line 8 – Type in "The untold Story of Mahavatar Babaji, the Yogi…" on youtube.com Mahaavatar Babaji found here – Link here https://www.youtube.com/watch?v=oJD6H-ujnl0

19. SEE LOG OF MEDIA # 4

20. Page 88 – Line 26 – Video by author type in on youtube.com "Becoming friends with Infinity by Joseph Vertino" Link here : "Becoming friends with Infinity" *by Joseph Vertino (youtube) please watch and SHARE - https://www.youtube.com/live/O6qevv_W0Ik?si=L9SvG17_4fCg7GJT

21. Page 90- Line 25- Type in on youtube.com "Eckhart Tolle in Conversation with Dog Whisperer Cesar Millan"- Link is here

22. Cesar Milan and Eckhart Tolle – interview – video here: https://www.youtube.com/watch?v=wc8ZxIR-gjk

23. Page 98 – Line 17 – "Man's Eternal Quest" by Paramhansa Yoganada thee Ascended Master – LINK TO BOOK: https://www.amazon.com/Mans-Eternal-Quest-Paramahansa-Yogananda/dp/0876122314

24. Page 103- Line 3 – Artist : Charles Ives song: "Rememberance" Link to media: https://www.youtube.com/watch?v=xIyJI3u5Mf4

25. Page 109- Line 20 "The Tao te Ching" book by Chinese holy man Lao Tzu-https://www.amazon.com/s?k=lao+tzu+book+%22tao+te+ching%22&i=stripbooks&crid=URCGK485G3J4&sprefix=lao+tzu+-book+tao+te+ching+%2Cstripbooks%2C91&ref=nb_sb_noss

26. Page 110- Line 28- Satsang by Mooji- video : https://www.youtube.com/watch?v=jXDaEyOzHuA&list=PLJMhwXfIQ9qTsiykL-EwpAUrIl6a3OFHU

27. Page 112- Line – 10- Bobby Mcferrin – Video "day of song" youtube : https://www.youtube.com/watch?v=81uJZIF9TCs

28. Page 116- Line 22 LOG OF MEDIA: WEBSITE – FACEBOOK PAGE BY AUTHOR – "Healing Prayers" - https://www.facebook.com/healingthroughprayer

29. Page 120- Line – 16- Type in on youtube.com "CCR Melbourne- Fr Richard McAlear" – Link of Video on LOG OF MEDIA: https://www.youtube.com/watch?v=eF3Cz9u_Bec&t=215s

30. Page 121- Line 26 Type on youtube.com: "The Hidden Chamber of the Heart by Joe Vertino" - "Video link of thee author reading from "The Human Aura" book- "Hidden chamber of thee Heart" https://www.youtube.com/watch?v=VBNRMmdXqGw

31. Page 121 - Line 26 – type in on amazon.com "The Human Aura by Djwal Kul and Lord Kuthumi" – link to online here "The Human Aura" book by Lord Kuthumi and Djwal Kul- https://www.amazon.com/s?k=the+human+aura+book+%28english%29&i=stripbooks&crid=32YY1OZ5Q8V8D&sprefix=the+human+aura+-book+english+%2Cstripbooks%2C82&ref=nb_sb_noss

32. Page 131- Line 20- Search on Facebook.com "Joe H Vertino" then go to saved videos and find "satsang 4" Dr. Joe Vertino - author - his SATSANG (from back in the day alone in a room) https://www.facebook.com/joe.h.vertino/videos/3015938338519810

33. Page-135 Line - 24- Type in on youtube.com "Animals as Leaders – Physical Education" – Link Music band video by "Animals as leaders" song is "Physical Education" https://www.youtube.com/watch?v=0jpOBd949O4

Log of Media

34. Page 135- Line 25- Type in on youtube.com "Meshuggah- New Millenium Cyanide Christ+ Stengah + The mouth licking what you bled" – Link is here : https://www.youtube.com/watch?v=fP8p3y-0qTQg Meshuggah; band – several songs

35. Page 141- Line 3 type in on amazon.com : - "The Ancient Secret of the Flower of Life by Drunvalo Melchizedek" Link: https://www.amazon.com/s?k=drunvalo+melchizedek+the+ancient+secret+of+the+-flower+of+life&i=stripbooks&crid=1KY7PL3LUAP3U&sprefix=drunvalo+melchizedek+the+ancient+secret+of+the+flower+of+life%2Cstripbooks%2C97&ref=nb_sb_noss

36. Page 159- Line 19- Type in on amazon.com : "The Reiki Bible: A Guide to Reiki Living by Joseph H. Vertino" author book Link: https://www.amazon.com/Reiki-Bible-guide-living-ebook/dp/B08W3NTYXX

37. Page 159 – Line 19 Type in user name "andromedajoe811" Personal music; user name is "Joe HV" on SoundCloud.com- Link Authors instagram video link- "How Reiki is for Everyone" https://www.instagram.com/p/DEDDM0wykND/

38. Page 163 - Line 13- Type in on youtube.com : "Practicing Non Fear Teaching by Thich Nhat Hanh" – Link Thich Nhat Hanh - Buddhist Spiritual Teacher link: https://www.youtube.com/watch?v=ObfJ-fA9q3ho

39. Page 165- Line 10 – Type in on youtube.com : "Steven Seagull – The 33 all Japan Aikido Demonstration"- Link "Video Aikido demonstration of Steven Seagull" https://www.youtube.com/watch?v=D-Vs--uHf4sE

40. Page 165- Line 16 - Type in on youtube.com : "More than a practice : meditation offers benefits to police officers, victims" – Link here : Police Incorporate Meditation - video - https://www.youtube.com/watch?v=jyOUGEP62Bs

41. Page 170 - Line 30- Type in on youtube.com: "Proper perspective on Mental health by Joe Vertino" – Link here: Video from author called "Proper Perspective on Mental Health" https://www.youtube.com/watch?v=MY8AGxLZzzo&t=431s (sorry if you have to scroll to beginning)

42. Page 174 - Line 21- Video: Type in on youtube.com: "Emma Kirkby- An Evening Hymn" song by composer Henry Purcell – Link here: https://www.youtube.com/watch?v=Qjc0qug-1NQ

43. Page 179- Line 30 – Type in on youtube.com : "Positive and negative beliefs and how they shape our reality by Bashar" - Link here: Bashar- Channeled Entity - video on positive and negative beliefs - https://www.youtube.com/watch?v=xHwKgrsfkQo

Log of Media

INFO for images in this book: Thee images on chapters 6, 9, 10, 11, 12, 13, 14, 15, 17 are all from personal use. All the rest of the 32 are derived from **Bing** the online search engine – and are being used for crime-free purposes- perhaps the best – being this book ! YAY. All legal and fall under Creative Commons Use!

Images Info : each image appears at the beginning of chapter (not all chapters have images though)
GIVE CREDIT to IMAGES with people on them!
1. Page 4 (1st Chapter) Mother Mary thee Ascended master (with golden background) – page 4
2. Page 6 Bobby Mcferrin- Image (exemplary human)
3. Page 20- Maharaj Neem Karoli Baba- Indian Saint image
4. Page 32- Personal Image of yogi in action
5. Page 41- Image of Author- Dr. Joe Vertino-
6. Page 49- Teal Swan – professional Spiritual Guide's Art – image
7. Page 57- Image of St. Hildegaard von Bingen- praised in book
8. Page 65- image of Buddhist master Frederick P. Lenz
9. Page 84- image of Buddhist Monk in Ocher
10. Page 99 – Paramhansa Yogananda thee Ascended master image and quote
11. Page 114 – The Dalai lama – Buddhist Spiritual leader and representative.
12. Page 143 – Drunvalo Melchizedek – Spiritual Figure- image
13. Page 154- Dr. Mikao Usui – founder of Reiki the tradition- image
14. Page 172- Steffany Gretzinger – Musical artist – image
15. Page 78- "Teal Swan I honor with integrity- and hold in a positive light and use her name and etc. well in my expertise and own mind- to say not only this very book -may we be blessed henceforth!"

References

Hey,

    A) These segments/chapter are presented with just their number ex. "1: Being in Love" (is chapter 1 in table of contents), ok, thanks to all the people and technologies responsible throughout human history, thus ALL the references, yay

    B) The chapters appear once and then it implied because the references are in chronological order and there are then perhaps at least 2 references from the chapter which can be seen at the first chronological reference only!

1. Title Page (Dr.*) in Author name and "Reiki"- I am a Doctor of it and in it- It is the "Universal Energy"

2. **Chapter 1**: Being in Love- Mother Mary thee Ascended Master. "My Soul magnifies the Lord and my Spirit rejoices in God my Savior" from The Holy Bible New testament: Luke 1:46-56

3. **Chapter 2**: Understanding Being Human- "E.T. The Extra-Terrestrial" Film, director Steven Spielberg, release year 1982

4. "Bashar" Persian name for Messenger is a channeled being; channeler is Darryl Anka; name for race is Sessanni helpers of humankind- Bashar Communications is alive and well online (on our Earth)- since 1980's

5. "Drunvalo Melchizedek" – Spiritual Guide- very open sharer of knowledge with beautiful eyes.

6. Bobby Mcferrin- brilliant /vocalist- song from album "Medicine Music" release year: 1990 song : "Common Threads" very much injested by Author for a strong period of his life as a beautiful man.

7. Quote by Soren Kierkegaard Danish Christian Existentialist Philosopher – 1840 "With great freedom comes great anxiety"

8. **Chapter 3**: Feeling your feelings– Music band: "Rage Against the

Machine" Songs mentioned "Bulls on parade" and "Guerilla radio" from Album : "The Battle of Los Angeles" release year: 1999

9. Zen Master Rama – person of Interest- Spiritualist and powerful master – popular in my eyes and in my book- here, forever, amen

10. "The Nothingness of Love: A Buddhist Book of Poetry" Book by (Author) by Joseph H. Vertino – available (at least as an) E- book on amazon.com see LOG OF MEDIA (1)

11. "Sri Yantra" and Tibet – The great symbol for deep concentration and perhaps the most Buddhist nation- what a rhyme! Is like art and sacred geometry in one – and is very serious traditionally speaking-

12. "Jesus Christ" Holy and Wholly dramatic historical figure – what a blessing to behold!

13. "AMMA" an Indian Hugging Saint who is woman like Sri Anandamai ma – and The Lotus mantra is mentioned and translated! "Om Nam Myoho Renge Kyo"

14. **Chapter 4**: Animals as leaders. Reference to Chapter 22: Absence of "Self"

15. **Chapter 5**: (Blank)- "Wisdom tells me I am nothing, love tells me I am Everything and between these two my life flows." – Sri Nisargadatta Maharaj- Indian Saint around in the year 1897 – Helps the mind become blank

16. Another Indian Sage- Sri Ramana Maharshi and his lineage – Papaji and Mooji – aligned and aligning business

17. **Chapter 6**: Shadow- Teal Swan- thee Spiritual Catalyst- Also happens to be a Pleiadean Starseed- wonderful influence on everybody- and estute in knowledge of "The Shadow" – is a famous Spiritual Guide.

18. Song "Tu Lo Sai" Italian Art Song (Aria) by Torelli year: 1680 – Music that does not encite regression evolutionarily speaking.

19. "Jesus Christ Super Star" release year: 1970 it's a musical – it is not a joking/comical one but God is still elated at Children's Laughter, haha! Excerpt in LOG OF MEDIA (3)

20. **Chapter 7**: Guru. Image and mention of Maharaj Neem Karoli Baba and Krishna Das- lovers of God in certain – and certainty is very useful! We can say it has the ability to bring souls from Darkness toward Light!

21. Hanuman mentioned – the monkey God in Hinduism – Image on page 127 of book Chapter "34: Devotion"

22. LOG OF MEDIA song "Hope for Enlightenment" by Lama Gyurme and Phillipe Rykiel – Song is a complete package- it honors the Guru, it honors the reason for the Guru, it honors our aesthetics and enjoyment self-pleasure ethically, it honors togetherness can be shared, it honors proper aligned (ethical) tradition(s). what a home run; from the album "Real World Gold" release year : 2012 (highly recommended)

23. **Chapter 8**: Clarity on Religion. Line 10 LOG OF MEDIA * Author's personal music; soundcloud.com

24. **Chapter 9**: Power. Quote by Jimi Hendrix, famous Black genius resilient and good worker guitarist " When the love of power gives in to the power of Love the world will know Peace." Title of Book connotation here in this quote!

25. **Chapter 11**: Karma. The greatest saint(?) Neem karoli baba put into this great book – relatively simple in context of his great importance of this world and all it can possible offer!

26. "Just keep Quiet" quote by thee Ascended master Papaji – One of many and one thee only one- original stuff. Like every star shining we can sing to and about in the cosmic array. Mooji and Sri Ramana Maharshi- all the same lineage of wisdom and purity of mind.

27. **Chapter 13**: The Importance of Adventure. Mother Mary thee Ascended master mentioned about saving me from the lost-ness in Paris in highschool far from my homeland- according to the thoughts of students and adults alike on the vacation too.

28. Zen- a word used throughout human history always consistent and reliable a cherished potential that we can cherish in our own self- "to see clearly" thus its next word "reality"

29. **Chapter 14** : The question of morality. The Dalai Lama- great World influencer and positive Buddhist figure, greatly honored and praised – quote "Silence is sometimes the best answer" . A firm reminder to every soul.

30. **Chapter 16**: What is Love, really? Fred Rogers and his TV show – "Mr. Roger's Neighborhood" premier year : 1968 – he was born on Pittsburg Pennsylvania and was a superhero of a role model- I even visited the monastery he was almost a priest with! How cool what a guy to look up to- simply profound.

31. Mother Priorus quote " God gives us Pain se we remain humble." Personal experience of author- known Cloistered nun in charge of convent, also was a Leo like thee Author, I cried dearly in front her because of her open heart :)

32. Mother Mary thee Ascended Master- honesty of author reveals the he was sexually attracted to her throughout his earlier(?) life!

33. The Supreme being Babaji – premavatar thee ascended Master

34. Gangaji – Spiritual teacher, divine and beautiful female who has a video called "The heart can bare it all" this video is available in the LOG OF MEDIA. (youtube) * year she began teaching : 1990

35. **Chapter 18**: Soul-Love. Teal Swan – the Spiritual Catalyst's Art: image – glorious just like the healing rosary!

36. "Anahata" the Sanskrit word for heart- root language of India! Very awesome and home of Kriya Yoga.

37. **Chapter 19**: The Three Jewels. The 5 Reiki Principles – good practice practical and mystical for everybody no exceptions- understood fully by Dr. Joe Vertino (Author) see instagram (andromedajoe811) VIDEO IN LOG OF MEDIA – "HOW Reiki is for Everyone" by Author. *

38. Another LOG OF MEDIA – Zen master Rama's tape from youtube – wonderful choice both for him to record it and you to listen to it! *

39. Another LOG OF MEDIA ; Author's different book called "The Reform of the Education System" Link and information on there ! *

40. **Chapter 20**: Nature and its healing attributes. Drunvalo Melchizedek – great Spiritual Figure who is and will be known as a great aid to humanity- and was inviting us into a path of the heart wish encourages much wisdom and growth- the same path in this manifesto!

41. Awesome inspiring Catholic Saint figure Hildegaard von Bingen- used lovingly in this book for great purpose of revelation!

42. Drunvalo Melchizedek Heart meditation * VIDEO OF LOG OF MEDIA :

43. The book "The Serpent of Light" by Drunvalo Melchizedek – a wonderful purpose packed and insight ridden expose about our inevitable realm thee Earth! Published year : 2008

44. The Catholic Saint – Hildegaard von Bingen (image in beginning of chapter also) mentioned for her specific beauty inherent in the Author's eyes who can't say for certain- but the music and thee earth and all the planets and the gravity together and her, Hildegaard how lovely- was around in the year 1150.

45. Two LOG OF MEDIA entry's Author's music on soundcloud and Hildegaard von Bingen's music - *

References

46. Mother Mary thee Ascended master mentioned 61- Line 1- Mentioning says thee Author about his work- Hanuman, Maharaj Neem karoli baba, and in reference to the title and point of this entire book; quote by Maharaj is "Feed people and Serve people" and also connecting us to thee Earth is this way of God's will and Love for all of us; our species humanity! Maharaj the baba of India was around in the year 1950.

47. VIDEO: LOG OF MEDIA : Instagram video by thee Author "Connecting to the Earth" ADD Link and info

48. Matt Kahn, Teal Swan, Mother Mary, Eckhart Tolle, Adyashanti, and Mooji- Spiritual role models that give providence and obedience to the will of God which is great and has solid chance in people's lives with these role models accessible! My father (of thee author) is quoted having said "Hurt People hurt People"

49. Mooji quoted saying "The greatest healing is enlightenment." Student of Papaji, teacher of many- Spiritual Guide and fatherly lover of souls with his direction and advice for liberation!

50. VIDEO LOG OF MEDIA – "Self Love is the way home" youtube video by author- about positive shift in your (personal) lifetime!

51. Gojira; music band; lyrics from song: Esoteric Surgery; album: "The way of All Flesh" quote is "You have the power to heal yourself!" release year: 2008- pertains to self-empowerment .

52. TOOL; music band, song is "Parabol" from the album "Lateralus" year of release: 2001 quote is "All this Pain is an Illusion!" – anecdote of healing written- mention of frontman Maynard James Keenan.

53. Tomas Haake of Meshuggah (drummer and lyricist) ; Swedish Metal Band from album Koloss, song: lyrics used in book passage "Do not Look Down" release year : 2012 lyrics used in book passage; "Strive, strive – surmount the obstacles. Attain the essence of your goals." commentary about making fun of useless pursuits so as to

rid you of them.

54. The Dalai Lama, Spiritual Buddhist figure of mastery quoted saying "All people want to be happy and reverse suffering."

55. Osho the mystic mentioned – also an stronghold of mastery for the ages and all people- was Indian unlike the Dalai lama who was Tibetan – founded Rajneeshpuram which is still super awesomely popular because it was the decision of people. That's what you get for being (whispers*… authentic). Highly recommended!

56. **Chapter 22**: The absence of "self". Image of Dr. Frederick P. Lenz- a beautiful man you may stare at him I give you permission for he is good just to stare at- look he is beautiful like my writing , ah. Praised well in the passage- good guy!

57. Mooji's VIDEO: LOG OF MEDIA "Divine laughter" on youtube.com * explained in book.

58. "Awareness is not Seperation" youtube video by author VIDEO LOG OF MEDIA *

59. Quote "I only need God." By Maharaji Neem Karoli baba.

60. **Chapter 23**: Relationship(s). "The Energy Body" mentioned – is the same thing as "chakras" – divine wheels that enable and are enabled – just as we need to move they move but they only flow. Ultimately important! Also mentioned in this book is another historically important one called "The Human Aura" by Djwal Kul and Lord Kuthumi

61. Jesus Christ mentioned- thee Ascended master – that there is a connecting force found in the heart- in which we are when we empathize like with Jesus- his beautiful visage in our shared world makes that much easier and appropriate.

62. **Chapter 25**: Organized Religion and God. Book mentioned is "God

References

without Religion" published in the year : 2011- used for the point of true issues and also true resolutions in real life.

63. The Dalai Lama : The great Buddhist leader who is Tenzin Gyatso- the Ocean Guru! He is a strong leader an example of character and his lineage of love so to speak is responsible for order and clarity collectively, thanks!

64. Quote from the Gnostic Gospels "My (real) church is not made of sticks and stones." Jesus Christ made this to bring order and clarity to (all) souls. That God's omni-presence is greater than the potential sway of right and wrong that is lower than the Absolute right and wrong.

65. Maharaji, great Indian Saint and guru Ram das and Krishna Das, and babaji the premavatar and also Paramhansa Yoganandaji the Ascended master. These are all holy figures who are designated to be experienced by the collective of humanity.

66. VIDEO LOG OF MEDIA: – a very soulful and wonderful being who is of Indian heritage and provides we could say somehow to anyone God ordains to receive his grace anywhere in the world!- thank you God for him and his beautiful visage ! *

67. Maharaj- Neem Karoli Baba – Indian Saint- who is a dear father figure to anyone who comes to him in that way- which is very important to receive and be open to that love!

68. **Chapter 26**: Work and Discipline. "Starseeds" mentioned – a very sacred word – it means a being who is seeded from a specific star system or part of the cosmic array and this being incarnates as a human and this starry energy that was seeded is used by God to transmute pain and improve the current species they are- humans! Thee Author is One of these- I am an Andromedan!

69. Quote by father of author "I work to live not live to work" – commentary on contemporary realm of work – making a sociological

and ultimately personal point!

70. **Chapter 27**: Death. Ram Dass; a.k.a. DR. Richard Alpert written about – had a particular relationship with death based on his personal and shared experiences around drugs earlier in his life- then he clung to them and it feuled more of his wisdom and growth that he shared throughout his life! Babaji mentioned at the bottom of the page- who efficiently represents mastery inside of the average human being!

71. Lord Buddha- the Ascended master known as Siddhartha Guatama written In about his personal agenda of life in context of the great purpose of enlightenment!

72. VIDEO LOG OF MEDIA* : "Hope for Enlightenment" song by Lama Gyurme Buddhist monk and wonderful singer and collaborator

73. VIDEO LOG OF MEDIA *: "Becoming Friends with Infinity" by Joseph Vertino (Author)

74. **Chapter 28**: Pets, animals, creatures of all kinds. Matt Kahn, professional Spiritual Guide, like thee Author- provides wisdom that is founded, humble, and powerful but some would say most importantly it is heart-centered!

75. *Cesar Milan, the dog whisperer and Eckhart Tolle mentioned- a wonderful example of how two individuals can share vulnerably – and having obtained helpful success to boot! VIDEO LOG OF MEDIA (following) * Interview between them!

76. Jesus, Mother Mary, and St. Joseph mentioned the Holy Family- exercise given of inviting God into your surroundings in your life so that you can be surrounded by God and even though you may not know everything about the people around you- You are welcome to recognize them as capable of being saintly and possessing Love and affection (potentially for everyone).

77. Peter Parker of Spiderman hero in the comic mentioned in context of expanding our consciousness and what a wonderful way of life- these topics, items, heroes come into our life and we can use them to evolve better!

78. Drunvalo Melchizedek – very holy and loving figure who is clear in his assistance consistently to humanity and helps bring the beauty to the forefront of our minds, Thanks Mr. Drunvalo Melchizedek

79. **Chapter 29**: Divine Relationships. Book : "Man's Eternal Quest" by Paramhansa Yogananda A wonderful text that was all-around vibrant and an impeccable invitiation into the here-to-fore-unseen realms of divine awareness, Year released: 1975 Publisher : Self- Realization Fellowship.

80. **Chapter 30**: Angels and spiritual guides. Mary pregnant with Jesus – Archangel Gabriel very clearly historically associated with the birth- and further proof how angels are really invested in human history.

81. The three Tenors – Pavarotti, Domingo, and Carreras famous men for vocal performance who are highly revered and guarded in the halls in our shared world. How prevalent a tradition Music is in our divinely inspired species.

82. "The Little Mermaid" Animated Film by Disney, released year: 1989 – used to exemplify and raise up our sights on ourself our self-image and to compare our names to those of Archangels!

83. 25 VIDEO LOG OF MEDIA song by Charles Ives, musical composer, American man, song" "Rememberance" a very touching tune relating to Fateful memories of our Father's. release year : 1919

84. **Chapter 31**: Different Religions and their purpose for our future Page 108- Line 8 "For the fruit of the Spirit is Love, joy, Peace etc…" quote from the Holy Bible Galatians 5: 22-23 New Testament . A

piece of wisdom that is all-embracing in its scope because we have its setting forever in our souls- the meaning of this quote is found over and over again in our development!

85. Drunvalo Melchizedek and Jesus – important divine masculine figures throughout our human history.

86. Lao Tzu is a Chinese Spiritual Mystic who has transcended much that he has achieved greatness and is worldly- renowned for this which is hugely obvious, clear, and simple- I pray this direct means of clear seeing prevails!

87. "The Tao te Ching" book by Lao Tzu – written in the year 400 B.C. and quote from the beginning of the book there "The Tao that can be spoken is not the eternal Tao."

88. Mooji spiritual guide excellent for the masses and easy to take seriously, hahaha, Sri Ramana Maharshi- an Indian Saint who was connected to Pure Consciousness.

89. Professional vocalist – Bobby Mcferrin mentioned he is great at healing people with his gift in the way we are all meant to be – with our complete self that involves all of who we are as an individual! VIDEO LOG OF MEDIA*

90. The Dalai Lama; Buddhist positive influencer- talking about kindness and sharing the understanding we are all about and is all about us.

91. Dr. Mikao Usui- founder of the Reiki way and was a Leo just like thee author.

92. Quote from the Holy Bible "Only those who are like little children may enter the kingdom of heaven." Matthew 18: 2-5 New Testament

93. Father Richard Mcalear Charismatic healing Priest – wonderful soul and I can sense he has a deep devotion- had he is old now, highly recommended to foster growth, self-esteem, and to allow the Trust

in the Lord to manifest. His book "The Power of Healing Prayer" is mentioned in this work and is included in LOG OF MEDIA *

94. "If your eye be single, your body be full of Light" quote from the Holy Bible: new Testament Matthew 6:22

95. The Holy Bible quote "Moses went into the desert to raise up the serpent [of light]." New testament book of John 3: 14-21

96. Line 16 Mother Mary thee Ascended Master mentioned when she brought flame of Spirit into the others and it is depicted as the holy spirit resting above their heads- and is sustained in the Lord's will and is a grace to begin it there on you (all).

97. The Great White Brotherhood a.k.a Thee Ascended Masters are written in here and mentioned by name, also the cool word chohans and the 7 rays of rainbow awareness. Book mentioned of great import The Human Aura" written by Djwal Kul and Lord Kuthumi in LOG OF MEDIA * year published : 1970

98. **Chapter 33**: Spiritual Entities and how they matter to you. TV media mentioned very dramatic examples "The Exorcist" a horror film year released 1973 and ethically sound and productive TV show "Touched by an Angel" year released : 1994 Wonderful shows that were around when I was a child- used to give well enough knowledge on this exciting topic of Spiritual Entitites and our very life.

99. St. Padre Pio the Saint and Catholic Priest heavily assosciated with demonology and Stigmata exemplary in context of being a human. We have a beautiful statue of him that is golden in Buffalo, NY @ St. Margaret's Church.

100. Steven Gray also known as Adyashanti – Spiritual Guide with a grand and direct way forward with wisdom – but it is good that meditation is mentioned in this chapter – to properly abide and yet also seek the Truth is essentially Logical- for they are distinct in their operations.

101. Mother Mary thee Ascended Master – and the rosary her trademark and our prayer ritual – well- it is good to be certain of something and understanding that our mind is our own business. Image for Chapter 1: Being in Love

102. The movie "The exorcism of Emily Rose" horror movie involving demonic activity which is very dramatic and a psychological study in the sense that the human being is what we are what our reality is- and never a demon- so what is all these angles of ourself we can learn about from this (kind of) movie. Year released : 2005

103. Chapter 34: Devotion."My Heart tells me I am everything, my wisdom tells me I am nothing, between these two my life flows…" quote by Nisargadatta Maharaj- Indian holy man with eyes that bring up fires in souls to closen to thee I AM. Died in 1981

104. (Green Tara) Avalokiteshvara, the Buddhist deity of Compassion- It is important to know oneself and we are in danger if we do not see gentleness with our journey.

105. Sistine Chapel by Michelangelo ; a beautiful representation of the human and divine by both its creation with our free will and also its depiction of God – this type of focus is the passion of Devotion in us all! Manifested/created in the year : around 1500 in the Vatican buildings in Italy!

106. Chapter 35: Advaita Vedanta/Non-dual spiritual teachings and teachers. Spiritual Guides abounding of the likes of Mooji, Adyashanti, Francis Bennet, Papaji, and Gangaji- all beings that are strong of personality and are in the business of everyones business of our souls properly attaining Enlightenement.

107. Satchitananda * is a Sanskrit term that describes the ultimate reality of existence, consciousness, and bliss. It is a common theme

in Hindu and yogic philosophy, and is often interpreted as a state of consciousness to be attained. Line-28 Neem Karoli Baba and Sri Ramana Maharshi – two of the greatest figures to stare at throughout all time and space !

108. "The reason troubles happen is for one reason; people haven't learned to sit in a room and be happy with nothing." quote by Blaise Pascal, Philosopher – around the year : 1647

109. Video LOG OF MEDIA by author called SATSANG *

110. Maharaj Neem Karoli Baba and Sri Ramana Maharshi mentioned great indian saints and even more with (line 30) Adyashanti- Spiritual Guide, author, and proper path provider for souls of Liberation- the objective aspects of the "primarily" subjective realm of Spirituality including Enlightenement are witnessed and shared wisely and directly by Adyashanti - became popular around the year : 1996

111. **Chapter 36**: Attaining and generating balance. "Animals as Leaders" Tosin Abasi's favorite band Meshuggah is also thee author's! – wonderful these two metal bands I saw in concert also. It is very special to be present and this cool musical reference and instrumental band name "Animals as leaders" thee concept allows me to be more present – and have better balance.

112. Tomas Haake- the drummer and lyricist of Meshuggah – lyrics borrowed "The struggle to free yourself from restraints becomes my very shackles." From the song "disenchantment" from the album Catch thirty three.

113. "There will be Peace in the world when there is peace in the nations, there will be peace in the…" quote from Confucius; Chinese educator. He was around in the year of 5000 B.C. E.

114. "The Ancient Secret of the Flower of Life" by Drunvalo Melchizedek – year published : 1999 in LOG OF MEDIA.

115. Jesus, Buddha, Melchizedek, and Drunvalo Melchizedek (his image on Page 144 for the Chapter 38: The Importance of Self-Expression)- names used there- all very powerful and inspiring to us humans- along our path of the soul- onward it goes.

116. 30 Book "The Ancient Secret of the Flower of Life" by Drunvalo Melchizedek – year published : 1999 in LOG OF MEDIA.

117. Eckhart Tolle, the spiritual guide; in context of dealing with the Pain Body... he is an expert and God is so efficient that his one singular pain has already occurred and then his teachings enable and prevent people from pain- see efficiency. He became famous in 2000.

118. Dr. Frederick P. Lenz/ Zen master Rama- Sacred Buddhist Guide – became popular in the year 1982.

119. **Chapter 38**: The Importance of Self- Expression. "Lightworkers" a brilliant (pun there) term that is steeped in wisdom – simply a person who is adamant along their own path to work with Light and shine.

120. "Starseed" a serious but light-hearted term- Yahweh approves- mentioned more than once in this book- is cosmic help from the stars and we are aware of a deep peace says these starseeds- and may the help abound.

121. Buddha and Jesus – Awesome ancient figures who are representative of clear and accurate self-expression! Figures who properly represent how to achieve that goal consistently – we can say the defeat of the fear of being devoted to fully assisting other souls!

122. **Chapter 39**: The Importance of Beauty. Thee Ascended master – around in the 1920's – I discuss his energy his effect- and see him a/ one of my guru's- says Dr. Joe thee Author.

References

123. **Chapter 40**: Government. "The Philosopher King's" idea given by Plato thee Greek Philosopher! Around in the year 380 B.C.E.

124. **Chapter 41**: Reiki Healing. "In Lacesh" a term which means the divine in me bows to the divine in you- a very collectively useful term to be official with!

125. Dr. Mikao Usui, Karuna, Tummo, and Holy fire Reiki- all mentioned in this book there – these are things at least generally associated in human collective's mind with benevolent people and energy medicine- it being of the intention to help us. And the tradition of Reiki – Usui being the most important (one).

126. The Lotus Mantra "Om Nam Myoho Renge Kyo" is present in this chapter and rings beautifully true in it (especially*)

127. Thee Ascended Masters – the liberated souls who help liberated all souls are written in this book- and are certainly on the same "team" as Reiki and would find some common ground with the human energy body as the focus… and knowledge as a great guarantee so to speak!

128. BOOK LOG OF MEDIA AND ALSO A VIDEO: "The Reiki Bible: A guide to Reiki Living" and also video: "How Reiki is for Everyone" (both by author)

129. Pine Bush NY, Buddhist grounds called Plum Village assosciated with Thich Nhat Hanh- Vietnamese Buddhist World Leader … man was born in 1926

130. Jesus and the order of Melchizedek mentioned – order is something that cannot be denied generally and is so welcomed in martial arts. It also encourages faith.

131. **Chapter 42**: Martial Arts. Mentioned of Tae Kwon Do, Karate, and Muay Thai, Kung Fu, and Wushu – all different styles from different cultures and it is good to look into what is the same in them and what is different in all of them!

132. "The Quest" movie release year : 1996," Mortal Kombat" release year: 1992, "Street Fighter 1 and 2" release year : 1987 and 1991, "Cyborg" release year: 1989 "Ip man" release year: 2010, "The Last Samurai" release year: 2003.

133. 25 LOG OF MEDIA : Steven Seagull Aikido demonstration VIDEO and Line LOG OF MEDIA VIDEO: Police incorporating meditation Line 25.

134. **Chapter 44**: Mental Conditions and Altered Perspectives. "When the power of Love overcomes the love for power the world will know Peace." Quote by Jimi Hendrix, professional guitarist from the past – popular in the 1970's How good is it to have someway to aim your life- thanks Jimi Hendrix, sir!

135. VIDEO in LOG OF MEDIA ; Youtube by Joe Vertino (author) "Proper Perspective on Mental Health"

136. **Chapter 45**: Music. Henry Purcell musical composer mentioned and great song available in LOG OF MEDIA – "An Evening Hymn" * - "If Music be the Food of Love ..." lyrics from a different song same composer (line 21).

137. Bobby Mcferrin – famous African American singer and improvisationalist. Very good at skat*

138. Henry Purcell-classical composer from the year 1680- song mentioned "If Music be the food of Love, sing on…"

139. The Holy Bible quote " God spoke and Light was made" from Genesis 1:3 (first book)

140. **Chapter 46**: Honor. 10 VIDEO LOG OF MEDIA : Bashar- Youtube video on positive and negative beliefs.

141. **Conclusion**. Ram Dass (Spiritual Guru) Dr. Mikao Usui (founder of Reiki tradition) and Mother Mary thee Ascended Master all mentioned in closing prayer – directed to the Lord of Love (what beautiful color I put in the text).

www.ingramcontent.com/pod-product-compliance
Lightning Source LLC
La Vergne TN
LVHW021805060526
838201LV00058B/3241